W9-CLR-571

BOOKS BY M. A. DEWOLFE HOWE

AUTHOR

Boston, the Place and the People

Life and Letters of George Bancroft

The Boston Symphony Orchestra

The *Atlantic Monthly* and Its Makers

Memories of a Hostess [Mrs. James T. Fields]

Barrett Wendell and His Letters (PULITZER PRIZE FOR BIOGRAPHY)

Bristol, Rhode Island: A Town Biography

Semi-Centennial History of the Tavern Club

John Jay Chapman and His Letters

Holmes of the Breakfast-Table

A Venture in Remembrance

Boston Landmarks (WITH PHOTOGRAPHS BY SAMUEL CHAMBERLAIN)

Who Lived Here? (WITH PHOTOGRAPHS BY SAMUEL CHAMBERLAIN)

AND OTHERS, INCLUDING FIVE BOOKS OF VERSE

EDITOR

Home Letters of General Sherman

Later Years of the Saturday Club

New Letters of James Russell Lowell

The Articulate Sisters

AND OTHERS, INCLUDING 31 VOLUMES OF "BEACON BIOGRAPHIES"

WHO LIVED HERE?

Doorway — Emily Dickinson House

WHO LIVED HERE?

A Baker's Dozen of
Historic New England Houses
and Their Occupants

Text by
M. A. DeWOLFE HOWE

Photographs by
SAMUEL CHAMBERLAIN

Boston
Little, Brown and Company · 1952

COPYRIGHT 1952, BY M. A. DE WOLFE HOWE AND SAMUEL CHAMBERLAIN

ALL RIGHTS RESERVED. NO PART OF THIS BOOK IN EXCESS OF FIVE
HUNDRED WORDS MAY BE REPRODUCED IN ANY FORM WITHOUT
PERMISSION IN WRITING FROM THE PUBLISHER

LIBRARY OF CONGRESS CATALOG CARD NO. 52-5872

FIRST EDITION

F
3
H 853

32615

*Published simultaneously
in Canada by McClelland and Stewart Limited*

PRINTED IN THE UNITED STATES OF AMERICA

Note

THE COLLABORATORS in the production of this volume would dedicate it to each other. The author has left to the illustrator all coverage of the houses with which the book is concerned. The illustrator has left to the author all peopling of his unpeopled houses with their inhabitants. In this conjunction of picture and biography, author and illustrator hope alike that the other may win some advantage from his fellow's contribution to the following pages.

M. A. DeW. H.

S. C.

Contents

List of Illustrations

xi

LIST OF ILLUSTRATIONS

LIST OF ILLUSTRATIONS

WHO LIVED HERE?

The Adams Mansion — Quincy, Massachusetts

The Adams Mansion — Garden Façade

I

Adamses at Quincy

IT MUST have been that I read the *Autobiography* of Charles Francis Adams, published in 1916, before reading *The Education of Henry Adams*, made generally accessible in 1918. On the flyleaf of that second book I find that I wrote, no doubt immediately upon reading it, the following lines, applying perhaps more accurately to the first of these two books than to the second:

> In Adam's fall
> We sinnéd all,
> And ever since that maladroit beginning
> Against the Adamses the world's been sinning.

Through all the merits of each of these autobiographies — and the merits of the *Education* place it in the front rank of American works of its kind — there is a pervading sense of grievance against the general order of things surrounding the two brothers. Though it cannot escape a reader's notice that each of them found a liberal share of enjoyments and rewards in his life, each records a series of mistakes, failures, and disappointments. Their younger brother Brooks abstained from autobiography, but his writings in other fields suggest a kindred sense of discouragement. When the First World War was beginning, in 1914, I remember asking him, as we were all asking one another, how long he thought it would last. "Oh," he replied, "allowing for temporary truces, I should say about thirty years." In the 1940's I remember also noting how accurately this characteristic prophecy had been fulfilled.

These three and their elder brother, John Quincy, were the last of the Adamses, in the fourth generation from the first President of the name, actually to live, either in boyhood or in maturity, in what their family called "the Old House." Since it was given in 1946 with all its contents — personal, historical, American, European — to the United States Government which now maintains it generously, through the National Park Service, as a shrine, it has been called "the Adams Mansion." Only one of the brothers, Charles Francis, had much to do with practical affairs, yet this did not exclude him from the brotherhood of scholarship and writing. An equal vigor in the written and the spoken word was a recognizable Adams trait. It has even been told that a younger member of the family, sitting directly in front of President Eliot, more than fifty years ago at a football game in Cambridge, was urging a Harvard player, with imprecations then unprintable, to run his damnedest for a touchdown, and thus provoked the deep-voiced Eliot to exclaim, "Spoken like a true Adams!" Joined with the sense of grievance which both

Presidents of the name brought back to Quincy from Washington when their terms of office ended, the gift of vigorous utterance may well have been transmitted, though in altered terms, to the generations that followed.

In any survey of historic houses and their occupants, each house is generally found to derive its importance from its association with one person. The Adams house at Quincy stands alone in having sheltered distinguished persons of the same name in four immediately successive generations. It is remarkable enough that the second and sixth Presidents of the United States, our Minister to Great Britain who kept that nation from siding with the Confederacy in our Civil War, and might himself have been another President — though only of Harvard — had he so chosen, and such men of thought and action as the Minister's four sons should have belonged to a single unbroken line. It is equally remarkable that all of them in turn lived in the same house. There are men of one book, and houses of one man. Such, obviously, is not the Adams Mansion at Quincy.

There is nevertheless an element of unity to be found in any consideration of this house. Of all private houses in America it has probably been the one in which the greatest force of constructive thinking and writing has been generated. This may seem an extreme statement, but one can make it without fear that another house so inhabited and so remarkable for its products in the field of intellect can be named in confutation. So it must be regarded not merely as a dwelling place of men but as a house and home of thought.

The oldest portion of the house was built in 1731 by Major Leonard Vassall of a prosperous Tory family with a fortune based on trade between Boston and the West Indies. The lines of Dr. Holmes in "The Cambridge Churchyard":

> There stand the Goblet and the Sun,
> What need of more beside?

recall the shameless pun of the Vassall family crest, a Vase and Sol. In 1787, John Adams, then serving as our first envoy to the Court of St. James's, acquired the house from Leonard Vassall Borland, a grandson of its builder. When his wife Abigail returned from London in 1788, fresh from the ample dwelling-places of France and England, she was appalled by the smallness of their new abode, and wrote to her daughter, "In height and breadth it feels like a wren's house." She advised this daughter, who had married a secretary of Washington's in the Revolution, to wear no feathers — "and let Colonel Smith come without heels to his shoes, or he will not be able to walk upright."

John Adams named the house "Peacefield," through memory of his Peace Treaty labors in Paris before going to London, but his immediate occupations in America, first as Secretary of State and then as President, removed him from Quincy for large portions of every year, until his Presidency came to an end in 1801. From that time until his death in 1826 he lived in the Old House. As early as 1800 he had satisfied his wife's desire for more space by building, at the opposite end of the house from the room Major Vassall had paneled with San Domingo mahogany, the so-called Long Room on the ground floor and his own spacious study above it. In successive generations further extensions have been made. The "wren's house" has become indeed a Mansion. In its rear the ample garden, with its box-lined paths, is maintained in the very form devised by Major Vassall.

In the published writings of John Adams, the letters he wrote from the Old House testify especially to the activity of the mind of its master. When his son John Quincy, at eighteen, was on the point of returning from Europe in 1785 to enter Harvard, a letter from John Adams to Professor Benjamin Waterhouse suggested the quality of mental equipment with which the father undertook to provide the son. After relating the young man's own achievements in the humanities, especially Latin and Greek, he wrote: "In the Course of the last year, instead of playing Cards like the fashionable world, I have spent my Evenings with him." These evenings were devoted to mathematics and the sciences, from Euclid in Latin to "the Methods of Fluxions and infinite Series of Sir Isaac

Newton." He hoped his son would be "on his guard against those Airs of Superiority among the Scholars," to which "his manifest Superiority" might entitle him. After this parental preparation it is no wonder that John Quincy Adams, both as President and as Member of Congress, could employ the resources of a keen intellect trained in many fields, including those of science, far beyond the accepted limits of Americans in public office.

On his father's death, in the year after his own Presidency began, John Quincy Adams came into possession of the Old House. His duties in the White House and then in the House of Representatives, on the floor of which he was struck by death in 1848, prevented his constant occupancy of the house at Quincy. His affections for it and for his mother, Abigail Adams, who gave him the name of her grandfather John Quincy, were intimately blended. The warmth of heart and keenness of mind revealed in her letters are widely known. "While she lived," this son of hers wrote, after her death, "whenever I returned to the paternal roof I felt as if the joys and charms of childhood returned to make me happy; all was kindness and affection." According to his grandson Brooks, his love and veneration for his mother "even passed the adoration of Catholics for the Virgin." When doubts of his own immortality assailed him before his death, it was the memory of his mother, again according to his realistic grandson, that presented an obstacle to re-

The Parlor — Adams Mansion

The Presidential Office — Adams Mansion

The Dining Room — Adams Mansion

West Parlor — Adams Mansion

nouncing his own faith in a future life which he could not surmount. He is reported to have made a habit of reading five chapters of the Bible every morning, and repeating every night of his life the prayer, "Now I lay me down to sleep," taught him in infancy by his mother. If this be true, the influence of an Adams mother must surely be placed beside that of the Adams fathers.

From John Quincy Adams the Old House passed in 1848 to his only son, Charles Francis Adams. His marriage to a daughter of Peter Chardon Brooks, reputed the richest man in New England, contributed to the freedom, such as each of his four sons also enjoyed, to serve his time in his own way. It was a way, for him, that led to great advantage to his country, through his work as Minister to Great Britain through our Civil War and afterwards at Geneva at the arbitration of claims against England growing out of that war.

His winter home was in Boston, but to Quincy he resorted for long summers, to the great relief and delight of his four sons. There, before his most important public work began, he edited the *Works* of his grandfather, John Adams, in ten volumes, and, in 1870, built the Stone Library, separate from the Mansion, for the books that overflowed the house. Even now, with some thousands of John Adams's books in the Boston Public Library, and other thousands of John Quincy Adams's in the Boston Athenæum, the house is by no means bare of them, and the Stone Library holds still other thousands, including all the writings of four generations of the family. If any physical token could indicate the extent to which this Quincy dwelling-house has been a working place for the mind, those facts about the books would provide it.

Of the four sons of Charles Francis Adams, John Quincy and Charles Francis lived in the house only as boys. In manhood each had a large country place of his own in Quincy, and devoted himself in many ways to the interests of the town. John Quincy was not a writer of books, but a person of uncommon ability and charm, with an independence of spirit which caused him to break away from the Republican party after the Civil War and to lead the unpopular Democratic cause in Massachusetts when it stood no chance at the polls. Cleveland offered him the post of Secretary of the Navy later held by his son Charles Francis Adams, but his health had begun to fail and he declined it.

Of the three writing brothers — Charles Francis, Henry, and Brooks — Charles Francis, in spite of his pre-occupation with business as president of the Union Pacific Railroad and the Kansas City Stockyards, wrote prolifi-cally on many subjects — railroads, education, politics, and history relating especially to Massachusetts. As presi-dent of the Massachusetts Historical Society for twenty years he served the cause of historical writing in his time to an extraordinary degree. When he read the dictum of

THE ADAMSES

James Russell Lowell, in his *Letters* edited by Charles Eliot Norton, that "the Adamses have a genius for saying even a gracious thing in an ungracious way," he spoke to Norton of his keen satisfaction in the passage, and his sincere gladness that it had not been omitted. Norton showed "unconcealed embarrassment," but Adams, in his *Autobiography*, pronounced the dictum "so keen and true!"

Such acceptance of fact, or what passed for it, was a family characteristic. Henry Adams was in the prime of middle life when he spent several summers in the Old House and there worked on his *History of the United States during the Administrations of Jefferson and Madison* in nine volumes, which fixed his high place among American historians. His more popularly read single volumes, *Mont-Saint-Michel and Chartres* and *The Education of Henry Adams*, were the products of his increasingly self-scrutinizing years, and, especially in the *Education*, his appraisals of his own limitations were at their height. The detachment with which he could look upon himself and his world was further illustrated in the Letters abundantly published since his death.

His brother Brooks, youngest of the four, made the house his summer residence for a number of years before his death in 1927. Here much of his own writing, a blend of history, economics, and philosophy, was done. Like his brother Henry, he suffered no inhibitions in self-appraisal — even recording in print his warning to his future wife that, in view of his extreme eccentricity, her marriage with him must be undertaken on her own responsibility and at her own risk. The risk proved well worth taking.

Presumably in the Old House he wrote the address delivered at the 275th Anniversary of the First Parish Church, Quincy, on October 11, 1914. Near its beginning he admitted a suspicion that he was "not in sympathy with the easy optimism" of most of his countrymen. He went on to confess that in his opinion "no society like anything which we or our ancestors have known, can cohere without a faith in revealed religion"; and finally he declared, "Lord, I believe, help thou mine unbelief." So the eighteenth-century faith of his fathers found its twentieth-century expression.

Beyond all matters of detail the important point of this consideration of a single house and its successive occupants, fathers and sons of a single family, is that from 1787 to 1927, a span of one hundred and forty years, it provided the setting for personalities and intellectual activities of a scope and value that has been seen to set it quite apart from any other house in America.

The Wayside — Concord, Massachusetts

Orchard House in Winter — Concord, Massachusetts

II

Louisa May Alcott:
"Duty's Faithful Child"

BACK in the nineteenth century a lady of Philadelphia used to tell of an experience in Christmas shopping. She was seeking toys for her own and other children. When the salesman spread the season's wares before her, she exclaimed, "But these are nothing but the same old toys you have been showing year after year." "Yes, madam," came the reply, "but remember — there are always new babies."

So it has been, for more than eighty years, with Louisa M. Alcott's *Little Women*. There have always been new little girls to read this story of the author's own girlhood, so accurately autobiographical in a great variety of its details that the facts in the various accounts of her life and the fiction of *Little Women* are hardly distinguishable.

New babies, new little readers of the same *Little Women*, and back of both "the Newness," that strange New England phase of mind before 1850 in which the ferment of Transcendentalism played a vital part. Louisa's father, Amos Bronson Alcott, was one of its conspicuous figures, and "the Newness" entered prevailingly into the education of his four daughters.

Any comprehension of Louisa May Alcott involves some knowledge of her remarkable parents. Her father, Connecticut peddler, schoolteacher, all-round theorist in education and general reform, would have preferred the designation of philosopher. When Dr. McCosh of Princeton asked Louisa Alcott for her definition of a philosopher, she answered, "My definition is of a man up in a balloon, with his family and friends holding the ropes which confine him to earth, and trying to haul him down." Incorrigibly hopeful, he was not deterred by an early experience in delivering in the West those one-sided lectures which he called "Conversations" from carrying them to ultimate success. "So poor, so hopeful, so serene," Louisa described him as he set forth in 1853. On his return one night in February his family, housed in Pinckney Street, Boston, and roused by the ringing doorbell, rushed downstairs to greet him. "My husband!" cried Mrs. Alcott in delight. When "the half-frozen wanderer, who came in hungry, cold, and disappointed, but smiling bravely," had been embraced and brooded over by wife and all four daughters, the youngest, little May, asked, "Well, did people pay you?" He opened his pocketbook, took out one dollar, and with a tear-compelling smile said, "Only that! My overcoat was stolen, and I had to buy a shawl. Many promises were not kept, and travelling is costly; but I have opened the way, and another year shall do better." Whereupon his wife kissed him, saying, "I call that doing *very well*. Since you are safely home, dear, we don't ask anything more."

It is easy enough to poke fun at Bronson Alcott, as blandly indifferent to debt as his daughter Louisa was deeply distressed by it. Thoreau was his friend, and yet could remark that "rats and mice make their nests in him." According to the elder Henry James, Carlyle found him "a terrible bore," but the more authenticated definition of him by Carlyle himself was, "A venerable Don Quixote, whom nobody can laugh at without loving." Of all his friends there was none that he esteemed so highly as Emerson, and Emerson, with occasional reservations, took him perhaps more nearly at his own valuation than any other competent contemporary. At one point in his journal he described Alcott as "the most extraordinary man and the highest genius of the time." Elsewhere in the journal, with a burst of frankness, he found his friend "a tedious archangel." What Emerson answered to Alcott's inquiry, "If Pythagoras should come to Concord, whom would he ask first to see?" is, however, unrecorded.

So impractical a husband, of whom his wife once said, "Send him for a pail of milk and he will come home with a cow," must have been hard to domesticate. After twenty-four years of married life she noted that they had lived in twenty-two different houses, and six more moves were yet to come. It has been said of the Pilgrim Mothers that, besides enduring all the hardships of the Pilgrim Fathers, they had the Fathers also to endure. The Alcott Father must have provided a stiff endurance test, but his wife, Abigail May of Boston, the "Marmee" of *Little Women*, met it with the extreme patience and gallantry which sprang from the deepest love. She was a sister of Samuel J. May, Unitarian minister and ardent abolitionist, who, with other generous relations and friends, came to the financial aid of what Louisa called "the Pathetic Family" at moments of their greatest stress. Through all vicissitudes her devotion to Alcott, shared by her daughters, stood unshaken. If Louisa, writing at thirty-six to her mother, could toss into a postscript "Regards to Plato," it was no more than a fling of family humor.

When Louisa Alcott was born at Germantown, Pennsylvania, November 29, 1832, her father's birthday in 1799, he was teaching a school under the auspices of a Philadelphia Quaker, at whose death in this very year of 1832 the financial support of the school came to an end. Undaunted by this reverse, Alcott opened in Boston his Temple School, in the Masonic Temple on the Temple Place corner now occupied by R. H. Stearns and Company. It was a novel undertaking, in which a boy of six could discourse to visitors on the need of more spirit and less clay in the human compound, and offenders against

The Library — Orchard House

Louisa May Alcott's Room — Orchard House

discipline were called upon to punish Alcott instead of suffering punishment themselves. On Louisa's third birthday she was brought to the school, placed on a table, crowned with a laurel wreath, and charged with the dispensing of little cakes, one to each child. At the last, one cake and one child were left. Louisa would have liked that "remainder biscuit" dearly, but on her mother's injunction that it is always better to give away nice things than to keep them, she surrendered it to a little Peabody girl, and learned her first lesson in sweetness and self-denial. The school prospered for a few years, but when Alcott, far ahead of his time, began some instructions in the "facts of life" and admitted a Negro pupil, the enrollment dropped from seventy to ten, and this venture in education had to be abandoned.

Darker days were yet to come. The Alcotts, exercising in poverty the strictest economies of their vegetarianism, moved from Boston to Concord, with Emerson as a central friend. Was it good or bad luck that the fame of the Temple School and its methods had spread through printed praise and blame to England, where a group of social reformers established an "Alcott House" on the educational principles of the Temple School? Alcott must needs visit it, and the generosity of Emerson — this "tender and illustrious man," as Louisa called him — enabled him to do so. On his return to America he was accompanied by fellow-enthusiasts from England. One of them, Charles Lane, possessed the means for the acquisition of a farm at Harvard, Massachusetts, hopefully dubbed "Fruitlands." Here all the Alcotts, with Lane and several others, bent on living as a "Consociate Family," found themselves established in June of 1843, when Louisa was ten years old. Emerson, well disposed but skeptical, remarked, "They look well in July. We will see them in December." By that time the Fruitlands experiment was a demonstrated failure. The plainest of living and highest of thinking could not prevail over a complete lack of common sense in the conduct of farm and family life. The "Consociates" inevitably fell apart. When the Alcott family with their possessions were quitting Fruitlands on an ox-sled, a frostbitten apple fell on the untrodden snow. Thus leaving Fruitlands behind them, Mrs. Alcott said to her husband, "Don't you think Apple Slump would be a better name for it, dear?" In later years Louisa drew with some extravagance on her juvenile memories in telling the Fruitlands story in her paper, "Transcendental Wild Oats," and she applied the name of Apple Slump to the Alcott ménage in less tragic surroundings. Apples, however, continued to form a large part of the Alcott family diet, even as a bust of Plato usually fed their thoughts.

If the Alcott parents have figured more largely so far in these pages than their daughter Louisa, it is only because her life was so largely affected, even shaped, by theirs.

Her father was almost her only teacher. He brought his daughters up not only on *Pilgrim's Progress* but also with moral instruction fortified by poetry, spiritual and philosophic thought beyond the usual capacity of the young. Self-expression was encouraged, for example, by their mother's establishment of a "Family Post-Office," a medium for interchange, in prose or in verse, between parents and children of their thoughts on matters of mutual interest and concern. Louisa developed early a gift of storytelling, "frightening my sisters," as she said, "out of their wits by awful tales whispered in bed" — a prelude to the sensational stories of her earliest days of writing for money. The acting of plays in the domestic circle was another prelude — to Louisa's later wish to become a professional actress, her success in monologues from Dickens, and even her writing of a farce produced at the Howard Athenæum in its preburlesque days.

The hardships of the Alcotts in the few years after the collapse of Fruitlands cannot be recounted here. The skies brightened when the death of Mrs. Alcott's grandfather May brought her an inheritance which enabled her to buy a house in Concord. This was "Hillside," afterwards Hawthorne's "Wayside," and from that the Alcotts proceeded to "Orchard House," now a shrine of memory for Louisa rather than her father. It is maintained by the Louisa May Alcott Memorial Association. There is a touch of irony in the facts that Louisa came to dislike living in Concord — "with its dampness and worry" — and that the writing of her masterpiece, *Little Women*, was not done in Hillside, the scene of its action, but in the overlooking Orchard House. It may be well to remember, besides, that, with all her appeal to girls, she much preferred boys, and wished that she were one herself.

Little Women did not appear till 1868, when she was thirty-six years old, and some twenty years of apprenticeship had preceded it. Some small *Comic Tragedies*, unpublished till after her death, were written in 1848 when she was only sixteen. In the second chapter of *Little Women* the account of the Christmas presentation of "The Witch's Curse, an Operatic Tragedy" suggests why she withheld them from publication. Her first book, *Flower Fables*, appeared in 1855. She had then learned that she could earn money, and so help her family, always more rather than less in need. At first she was glad to pick up payments of five or ten dollars from her offerings to periodicals. She tried her hand at teaching children, and when James T. Fields saw one of her manuscripts, before he became editor of the *Atlantic Monthly*, he said, "Stick to your teaching, Miss Alcott. You can't write." It was only a little later that Lowell accepted the first of her contributions to the *Atlantic*, and the payment of fifty dollars for it seemed the opening of a new era.

She declared frankly of her family, "We are real 'Micawbers,' " and, dimly foreseeing a possible future fortune, proposed to "invest it in the Alcott Sinking Fund, the Micawber R. R., and the Skimpole three per cents." The longest early step towards becoming the substantial money-maker for her family followed the publication of her *Hospital Sketches*, based on the letters she had written from a military hospital at Georgetown, D. C., through six weeks of the winter of 1862–1863. As she revised her letters she called herself "Nurse Tribulation Periwinkle" and the hospital experience ended in tribulation indeed — a severe illness which caused her to write in later years, "I was never ill before this time and never well afterwards."

The popularity of *Hospital Sketches* led, however, to an increased demand from editors and publishers for her writings, and her pen, never diverted to any labor of the file, was plied with greater energy and profit than ever before. It took an intelligent publisher, Thomas Niles, of the Boston firm of Roberts Brothers, to see what Louisa Alcott could still do with her powers of observation and narrative. In May of 1868 he suggested her writing a story for girls. On July 15 she handed him the completed manuscript of Part First of *Little Women, or Meg, Jo, Beth and Amy*. It was essentially a domestic narrative. Meg was her sister Anna, Jo herself, Beth her sister Elizabeth, and Amy her sister May. As she described these so-called March sisters, Jo, in a relentless self-portrait, was far the least attractive of the quartette. The improvident father was kept discreetly in the background. Mrs. March, as the beloved "Marmee," is a loving portrait of Mrs. Alcott. Without a trace of sophistication, the story unfolds the daily doings of a happy family, nourished on ideals, and putting them into practice through days both bright and dark. The instant response of the public, and its long endurance as a juvenile classic, outweigh the objections of earlier and later critics who have questioned the place of the book in "literature." What it did for the fortunes of the Alcott family, not only by itself but through establishing its author for the rest of her life as one of the most "successful" American writers, is suggested by the estimate that before the end a million copies of her books had been sold, with abundant returns to herself. Her father had every reason for bringing his sonnet in her praise to its conclusion with the words, "Duty's faithful child."

Far from being a woman "of one book," a complete bibliography of her writings — many books and many more contributions in prose and verse to periodicals juvenile and adult — numbers two hundred and seventy items. Nor was she only a writer. Outside the field of authorship she could sign herself "Yours for reforms of all kinds." Abolitionism came first, woman suffrage and temperance later. Near the end of her life, when the homeopathy she had long accepted failed to improve her health, she turned for a time, but without success, to a mind cure then newfangled. One reform in herself — if reform it be — from spinsterhood to matrimony, she never achieved. "Liberty," she once wrote, "is a better husband than love to many of us." When her sister Anna married John Pratt and Emerson kissed the bride, that seemed to Louisa an honor that "would make even matrimony endurable."

In her prosperity she provided every comfort for her father and mother. The beloved "Marmee" died at Orchard House in November 1877. In succeeding summers her father rejoiced in receiving at that house the visitors to the Concord Summer School of Philosophy established in his honor. In March of 1888 he died, in the house in Louisburg Square, Boston, where, disabled by a stroke of paralysis, he had enjoyed a sitting room containing a revolving bookcase filled with his own writings. There Louisa, far from well herself, came frequently, and at the last, from what would now be called a nursing home at Roxbury, to visit the father, sister, nephews, and niece for whose benefit she was maintaining the house. Her presentiment that she was seeing her father for the last time on March 1, 1888, proved true. Chilled in the return drive to Roxbury, she fell seriously ill, and died on March 6, unknowing that her father had himself died two days before. Their birthdays were the same, and by almost the narrowest of margins they missed dying on the same day — Louisa in her fifty-sixth year, her father in his eighty-ninth.

Let it not be thought that the child of duty went without pleasures. To be sure, she took to heart an injunction in one of her mother's "Family Post-Office" letters, "Love your duty, and you will be happy," but she found many other sources of happiness — in nature, European travel, human relationships in short measure as well as long. Did she not take a certain pleasure in the Polish countess of whom she wrote to her father from Switzerland? This lady and her daughter, she said, had been reading her books, and "Madame says she is not obliged to turn down any pages, so that the girls may not read them, as she does in many books." Against that recorded encounter may be placed her later meetings with Oscar Wilde in New York, with Ellen Terry at the Papyrus Club of Boston, and other indications that her conception of social relations was not limited by the family life of the Marches.

One little entry in her journal seems to have escaped comment by her biographers. When the Prince of Wales visited Boston in October 1860, Louisa Alcott, with a friend named Fanny, saw him and his train trot over the Common in a review. The two young women — Louisa was nearing thirty — "nodded and waved as he passed, and he openly winked his boyish eye at us." Fanny, Miss Alcott felt obliged to record, "looked rather rowdy, and the poor little prince wanted some fun." Fanny or no Fanny, it should not be forgotten that Louisa Alcott and the future Edward VII once exchanged nods and a wink.

Whitehall — Middletown, Rhode Island

The Green Room — Whitehall

The Green Room — Whitehall

III

Bishop Berkeley at Whitehall

THE REVEREND JAMES HONEYMAN (or Honyman), minister of the Society for the Propagation of the Gospel in Foreign Parts, was in his pulpit at Trinity Church, Newport, Rhode Island, on Sunday, January 23, 1729, when a messenger delivered a letter to him. He opened it at once, and learned that the Very Reverend George Berkeley, Dean of Derry in Ireland, might land in Newport at any moment. Honeyman brought the service to a quick conclusion, and with his congregation proceeded to Ferry Wharf to welcome the famous Dean, who had sailed early in September from Gravesend with his young wife, her friend Miss Handcock, Smibert the painter, and two gentlemen, Dalton and James by name, traveling for pleasure, and stopping over at the Virginia port at which the ship had touched on its way to Newport.

Berkeley's wife was soon to present him with his first child. He wrote of her as one "whose humour and turn of mind pleased me beyond anything that I know in her whole sex." The fame of Berkeley as a philosopher must have meant as much in Newport as in any American town

— perhaps more than elsewhere. The town was bustling with prosperous commerce. Withal there was a leaven of intellectual activity capable of responsive quickening through the presence of a distinguished philosopher. His early writings, *A Theory of Vision*, *Principles of Human Knowledge*, and *Dialogues*, would have found competent readers in Newport if anywhere in the colonies. There may not have been many to grasp completely his great "New Principle" — *esse est percipi* — to exist is to be perceived, which is like saying that nothing exists but in the thought of it, an early assertion of the superiority of mind over matter. Yet where, if not in Newport, would this have been understood?

Berkeley, born in Kilkenny County, Ireland, March 2, 1685, was not quite forty-four years old when he landed in Newport. He had studied and taught at Trinity College, Dublin. According to a story of that period of his life he witnessed an execution by hanging, and after it induced a friend, an uncle of Oliver Goldsmith, to perform an experimental hanging on himself. When it was stopped just short of success, Berkeley, apparently already in clerical orders, is reported to have exclaimed, "Bless me, Contarini, you have rumpled my band!" Here was an empiricist indeed, ready to try anything.

In 1713 he made his first trial of London, where he was welcomed to the company of writers and wits who became the glory of their time — Steele, Swift, Addison,

Arbuthnot, Pope. It was Pope who ascribed "to Berkeley every virtue under Heaven." When Addison's *Cato* had its first production, Berkeley was among the friends who sipped with him the burgundy and champagne that kept his spirits up between the acts. When Swift's Vanessa was about to die, angry at the report of his marriage with Stella, she so identified one of the future Deans with the other that she made a last-minute change in her will, under which Berkeley instead of Swift became a beneficiary. These may seem trifling instances, but they serve to suggest the kind of social experience Berkeley could bring with him to Newport.

The trial of London led to the trial of Continental travel, in two tours, first as chaplain to a diplomat, then as companion to the son of an Irish bishop. Through this experience Berkeley's taste in all the arts was nourished and enlarged. Travel ended, the books that fixed his reputation as a thinker written and published, he turned from philosophy to concrete plans for human betterment — especially his Bermuda College project. It was this that brought him to Newport.

The "still-vexed Bermoothes" of Shakespeare still vexed the minds of later poets and others in England. To Berkeley Bermuda appeared the ideal place for the establishment of a college for the education of colonial candidates for the ministry of the Church of England, and also for the Christianizing of Indians. The project was so appealing that scholars of Trinity and gentlemen of England were prepared to join Berkeley in carrying it out. When he laid his plan before the Scriblerus Club dining at Lord Bathurst's house in London, the members rose to their feet exclaiming, "Let us set out with him immediately!" The realistic William Byrd of Virginia raised the objection that there were no Indians in Bermuda and that Berkeley would have to bring them as captives from the American continent before their Christianization could begin. This did not discourage Berkeley and his friends, some of whom made liberal subscriptions to his enterprise. The British government, moreover, voted a grant of twenty thousand pounds — unhappily never paid — for the project.

Berkeley had already been appointed Dean of Derry, and, even in those days of absentee office-holding, his going direct to Bermuda would have cost him the tenancy of this post, as, for some reason, his coming to the continental New World would not. He was actuated, besides, by a wish to establish a base of supplies in food and income for his Bermuda college. Therefore, after spending a few months as the guest of the Reverend Mr. Honeyman, he bought a farm of about a hundred acres adjoining the farm of his clerical host, a few miles north of Newport town, and built on it the house which he named "Whitehall" in token of his loyalty to the reigning family in England whose palace had borne that name. The house may now be found near the meeting of two pleasantly named thoroughfares, Paradise Road, running north from Newport, and Green End Avenue. Berkeley Avenue, from which Whitehall is entered, is a continuation of Paradise Road.

There were possibilities of Berkeley's acquiring land also on Fisher's Island and the Elizabeth Islands as further bases of supply for Bermuda, but the Whitehall farm was held sufficient for the needs which, in fact, never arose.

While Berkeley was living at Whitehall, for the better part of three years, he produced a substantial book, *Alciphron, or the Minute Philosopher* in "Seven Dialogues, Containing an Apology for the Christian Religion, against those who are called Freethinkers." This is counted among his more important works. The Platonic dialogues of which it consists involved a group of accomplished friends bearing such classical names as Alciphron, Euphranor, Lysicles, and Crito. The term "minute philosopher" was derived from Cicero. In the first of the dialogues Berkeley identifies this philosopher with the modern freethinker, as belonging to "a sort of sect which diminish all the most valuable things, the thoughts, views, and hopes of men. . . . Human nature they contract and degrade to the narrow low standard of animal life, and assign us only a small pittance of time instead of immortality." Against this sect the claims of religion, especially as shown forth in the Church of England, are strongly urged. The book is written with such charm as to be far from unreadable today. This is hardly the time or place for any detailed study of it. Let us see rather what specific relation it bore to Berkeley's stay in Newport.

The book begins with an obvious reference to the impending collapse of the Bermuda Project. "Events are not in our power; but it always is to make good use of even the very worst." Hence, for one "who unites in his own person the philosopher and the farmer," the recourse to writing "in this distant retreat, far beyond the surge of that great whirlpool of business, faction and pleasure which is called *the world*."

A modest eminence near Berkeley's house bore the name of "Honeyman's Hill." The Dean himself did not build, as he might have done, on a little hill of his own, but showed himself indeed a philosopher when he said — or is said to have said — "to enjoy the prospect from the hill he must view it only occasionally; if his constant residence were on the hill the view would be so common as to lose all its charm." His enjoyment of other scenes within easy reach from Whitehall appears more than once in the pages of *Alciphron*. Let one citation, from the beginning of the Second Dialogue, recall his surroundings: "After breakfast, we went down to a beach about half a mile off; where we walked on the smooth sand with the ocean on one hand, and on the other wild broken rocks, intermixed with shady trees and springs of water, till the sun began to be uneasy. We then withdrew into a hollow glade, between two rocks."

It was a long half-mile from Whitehall to the Sachuest beaches, here rendered doubly recognizable by the obvious reference to the adjoining "Hanging Rocks," a strange formation suggesting the open jaws of some gigantic beast, beyond the proportions of a "hollow glade," yet reputed, with the confirmation of the enduring name "Bishop Berkeley's Seat" to be the very spot on which parts of *Alciphron* were written.

It was not only with nature that Berkeley could commune to his satisfaction. Congenial human society was close at hand. In Newport, besides Honeyman of Trinity Church, there were Nathaniel Kay, a generous benefactor, Colonel Daniel Updike, and others of an intellectual bent, who, under the stimulus of Berkeley's influence, founded in 1730 the Literary and Philosophical Society through which the admirable Redwood Library and Athenæum of Newport came into being, even as the Boston Athenæum was later to owe its origin to a local "Anthology Society." Beyond Conanicut Island across the Bay was the Reverend James MacSparran, representing to the Narragansett Country the same "Society with the Long Name" which had sent Honeyman to Newport. Still farther away was the Reverend Samuel Johnson, of Stratford, Connecticut, with whom Berkeley's relations became the most intimate of all.

Samuel Johnson, yet to become the first president of King's (later Columbia) College, was a graduate of Yale. It was through his intimacy with Berkeley that Yale came to mean so much to the "Irish Plato," the visiting Dean. The fact that Johnson and other graduates of Yale in the Congregational ministry had sought and obtained ordination in the Church of England won for the Connecticut college a place in Berkeley's eyes above that of Harvard. Yale, he felt, was doing more of what he had hoped for the Bermuda College of his dreams. He had brought some two thousand books with him from England, and when he left Newport he entrusted a box of them to Nathaniel Kay for distribution among the students at Yale. This was but the beginning, for soon after returning to England he sent nearly a thousand volumes to the Yale Library. He had seen the Harvard Library just before sailing for home, and, partly perhaps because he found it less in need of enrichment than the library at New Haven, he despatched from England a smaller consignment of books to Cambridge. These, unhappily, were all destroyed when Harvard Hall burned in 1764.

But books were by no means the only gift to Yale springing from Berkeley's friendship with Johnson. The college received also the title to his Whitehall property, from the income of which a long succession of "Berkeley Scholars" has profited. This title is still held by Yale University, which in 1897 committed the use of the place,

Kitchen Fireplace — Whitehall

Northeast Chamber — Whitehall

under a long lease, to the Colonial Dames of America, which maintains it as a Berkeley shrine. With a fine confidence in the future, the lease was made to cover 999 years. The house, redeemed from the decay into which it had fallen, is now furnished precisely as it might have been in Berkeley's time, and on its walls hang contemporaneous prints of his less famous American and more famous English friends.

At Newport Berkeley often preached in Trinity, to congregations containing many besides Anglicans. The simplicity of his clothing recommended him even to the Quakers, and all must have welcomed his urging upon the Anglican clergy of New England a more sympathetic attitude toward Dissenters.

And where was the Bermuda Project? Never carried out, by reason in large measure of the British government's failure to provide the promised endowment of twenty thousand pounds. Berkeley, thus discouraged, returned to England, sailing from Boston September 21, 1736. There remains in America the group portrait of himself, and seven Newport companions, including his infant son and Smibert, who painted the picture — yet another treasured possession of Yale University.

Returned to his native Ireland the Dean of Derry became the Bishop of Cloyne, occupied himself with good works, and produced a considerable work, *Siris*, proclaiming tar-water a panacea for many physical and other ills

33

32614

of the human race. This is far less a matter of present concern than the visible tokens of his influence in America — especially in the field of education. At Newport there has been a Cloyne School for boys. The Gothic tower of St. George's School, visible from Whitehall, reared its head nearly two hundred years after Berkeley's stay in Newport, yet one may imagine what pleasure his Anglican eyes would have taken in foreseeing it. The also neighboring Episcopal church of St. Columba, with its graveyard of a singular English beauty, is called the "Berkeley Memorial." The organ he gave to Trinity Church in Newport is represented there in portions of the existing instrument. As if the benefactions to Yale already mentioned were not enough, one of its sumptuous new buildings perpetuates the name of Berkeley. Also at New Haven stands the Berkeley Divinity School of the Episcopal Church. The late Dr. Benjamin Rand of Harvard, besides enumerating most of these points, declares that both Columbia and the University of Pennsylvania, under their original names, were established on principles derived from Berkeley.

Of all that he ever wrote nothing is more familiar than the four lines:

> Westward the course of empire takes its way;
> The first four acts already past,
> A fifth shall close the drama with the day:
> Time's noblest offspring is the last.

BISHOP BERKELEY

What could be more fitting than that the habitation of the great western University of California, at the farthest possible continental remove from the Whitehall of Rhode Island, has Berkeley for its name?

IV

Anne Bradstreet: Tenth Muse

ANNE BRADSTREET and her husband Simon Bradstreet came to New England with John Winthrop in 1630. They lived for a few years at Newtowne (Cambridge) and then at Ipswich, before settling, near 1650, at what is now North Andover, Massachusetts. The first edition of the book that won her fame as "the Tenth Muse" was printed in London in 1650. Simon Bradstreet's first house at North Andover, burned to the ground in 1666, was promptly replaced by the house pictured here, and visible today on Osgood Street, North Andover, near its junction with Academy Road. It now belongs to the North Andover Historical Society. Since Anne Bradstreet died in 1672, she could not have written within its walls many of the poems included in either the first or the second (Boston, 1678) edition of her book. But in no other house still standing could any of her poems have been written, and it is a fortunate circumstance that any existing house can be associated with one who may properly be called the first American Woman of Letters.

For this title her qualifications were unusual. Her English background and American experience were those of

Anne Bradstreet House — North Andover, Massachusetts

not many New England pioneer women. For this reason they can hardly be considered typical, but it is truly significant that they were even possible. Her father, Thomas Dudley, Deputy Governor under Winthrop before becoming Governor himself, a man of substance and proved ability before leaving England, served there as steward of the Earl of Lincoln's estate, Tattershall Castle. Under his care in that capacity was a young Simon Bradstreet, who took the degrees of bachelor and master of arts at Emmanuel College, Cambridge, became Dudley's successor as steward for the Earl of Lincoln, and held the same relation with the Countess of Warwick when, in 1628, he married Dudley's daughter Anne, then sixteen years old. At eighteen, she sailed with her father and husband on the *Arbella* bearing Winthrop and his closest associates to the New World.

The women who came with their menfolk to civilize a wilderness stood in need of two possessions, health and piety, the one to cope with the physical hardships awaiting them, the other to bear them up with all the spiritual resources of a deep-seated religious faith. On the score of general piety Emerson recalled a happy saying about the settlers of New England, who had so much of it that they had to hold hard to the huckleberry bushes to hinder themselves from being translated. With the equipment of health Anne Bradstreet was but slenderly endowed. Her childhood and girlhood were passed in delicate health, and when she married she waited, most reluctantly, for the arrival of her first child.

> The Son of Prayers, of vowes, of teares,
> The child I stay'd for many yeares.

She had schooled herself well to resignation, as one of many fruits of piety. The consciousness of sin held an early place among them. She wrote of realizing it in a childish illness: "But as I grew up to bee about 14 or 15 I found my heart most carnall and sitting loose from God, vanity and the follyes of youth take hold of me." At 16 the Lord smote her with smallpox. In her affliction she confessed her Pride and Vanity, and the Lord restored her.

All this bears an intimate relation to the puritanism which caused the alienation of her circle from the Church of England, and led to the emigration in search of a new order. Freed from the old authorities of church closely linked with state, what set Anne Bradstreet apart from most of the emigrating women was her exposure, in the Earl of Lincoln's household, to books, the works both of earlier writers and of her own exciting contemporaries — and not only her exposure, but her response to it.

One thing to be remembered is that in the ruling class of the Bay Colony to which Anne Bradstreet belonged, the clergy held a powerful place, and that among the immigrants to New England even before 1640 there were, as Professor Morison has pointed out, about one hundred and fifteen graduates of the English universities — of course chiefly ministers — and that seventy-four of these were in the Massachusetts Bay Colony. Here was no mean nucleus of cultivated readers. Difficult, then, as the mere mechanics of living must have been for anybody of Anne Bradstreet's tastes and gifts, she could feel that her voice, though crying in the wilderness, would find some sympathetic hearers not too far away.

It was not till she had been twenty years in the Colony that her abundant writings through that period laid claim to any public attention — and that came to pass through no motion of her own, but through that of an admiring brother-in-law. Besides producing much verse and prose through that twenty-year period, she was not prevented by her health, always delicate, from producing children, to the final number of seven beyond her first-born Samuel. Of the entire brood she wrote in a later year:

> I had eight birds hatcht in one nest,
> Four Cocks there were, and Hens the rest,
> I nurst them up with pain and care,
> Nor cost nor Labour did I spare,
> Till at the last they felt their wing,
> Mounted the Trees, and learn'd to sing.

In many succeeding lines, printed after death, each bird is described.

In 1647 John Woodbridge, minister of North An-dover, married to Anne Bradstreet's sister, Mercy Dudley, went to England, carrying with him a manuscript volume of his sister-in-law's writings. There, without her knowledge, it was printed in 1650. The book's full title page would demand more space than is here available. Thus it began and ended:

The
Tenth Muse
Lately sprung up in America,

OR

*Severall Poems, compiled
with great variety of Wit
and Learning, full of delight.*

. . . . .

By a Gentlewoman in these parts

Printed at London for Stephen Bowtell at the signe of the
Bible in Popes Head-Alley. 1650

Between these first and last lines there are others, describing the contents of the book. Much of it falls far short of revealing the author at her best, since it consists of long poems on the four Elements, Constitutions, Ages of Man, Seasons of the Year and the Four Monarchies, Assyrian, Persian, Grecian, Roman — almost as if in anticipation of Arnold Toynbee. She seems to have been infatuated with the figure four. In their substance these poems make an impressive show of learning, or at least of plentiful derivation from Sir Walter Raleigh's *History*

The Salt-Box Aspect of the Anne Bradstreet House

The Parlor – Anne Bradstreet House

Paneled Room – Anne Bradstreet House

of the World, Plutarch, the Bible, and other such sources. In form they have been found to owe too much to the once admired and now forgotten Guillaume du Bartas, translated by Joshua Sylvester. Anne Bradstreet's own admiration of Du Bartas is declared in her long poem in his honor, containing these two lines:

> Oft have I wonder'd at the hand of Heaven
> In giving one what would have served seven.

The London title page contained one further line that must be cited: "With divers other pleasant and serious Poems." In this category, which should be extended to include the prose *Meditations* she wrote for her son Simon, the best of Anne Bradstreet is to be found, whether in the London 1650 volume, or in "The Second Edition, Corrected by the Author and enlarged by an Addition of several other Poems found amongst her Papers after her Death" (Boston, 1678).

Woodbridge's Introduction to the Tenth Muse suggested that "the Reader should pass his sentence that it is the gift of women not only to speak most but to speak best," and in a poem to his "dear Sister" modestly named himself her "silly Servant," standing in the Porch, "Lighting your Sunlight with my blinking Torch." Introductory verses by others, including, in the second edition, James Rogers, president of Harvard, hailed the author as both woman and poet. She herself made early assertions of feminism.

WHO LIVED HERE?

I am obnoxious to each carping tongue
Who says my hand a needle better fits,
A Poets pen all scorn I should thus wrong,
For such despite they cast on female wits;
If what I do prove well, it won't advance,
They'll say 'tis stol'n, or else it was by chance.

This is in the Prologue to her "Four Elements"; and in the poem honoring Queen Elizabeth:

She hath wip'd off th' aspersion of her sex,
That women wisdom lack to play the Rex.

. . . .

Nay Masculines, you have thus tax'd us long
But she, though dead, will vindicate our wrong.

Puritan *bas bleu* as Anne Bradstreet may have been, it would be quite a mistake to recall her as nothing more. Due allowance should be made for her brother-in-law's summary of "her gracious demeanour, her eminent parts, her pious conversation, her courteous disposition, her exact diligence in her place, her discreet managing of her family connections." In her writings one may find at this late day direct evidence of clear and vigorous thinking, and of genuinely poetic expression.

Her prose *Meditations* written for her son Simon — seventy-seven in number, with four added in Latin — look back to Solomon and forward to Ben Franklin. Here is one of them: "It is reported of the peakcock that priding himself in his gay colors, he ruffles them up; but spying his black feet, he soon lets fall his plumes, so he that glorys in his gifts and adornings, should look upon his Corruptions, and that will damp his high thoughts." But it was in poetry rather than in proverbs that her real distinction lay.

Take, for example, "The Flesh and the Spirit," ending with lines about the Celestial City in which the Spirit dwells — a rendering in telling verse of a familiar passage in the Book of Revelations. Or look, still more attentively, at the long poem, "Contemplations," which first saw the light in the second edition of her writings. Nature was here her theme — the woods, the river, and all the outdoor objects to which she turned from her books. Chiefly of a high seriousness, its stanzas held touches of light fancy — as here:

> I heard the merry grasshopper then sing,
> The black clad Cricket bear a second part,
> They kept one tune, and plaid on the same string,
> Seeming to glory in their little Art.

With Addison and Shelley still to come, she wrote this stanza:

> When I behold the heavens as in their prime,
> And then the earth (though old) stil clad in green,
> The stones and trees, insensible of time
> Nor age nor wrinkle on their front are seen;
> If winter come, and greenness then do fade,
> A spring returns, and they more youthful made;
> But Man grows old, lies down, remains where once
>   he's laid.

And in conclusion this stanza, comparable with the best poetry of her own and later times, is found:

> O Time, the fatal wrack of mortal things,
> That draws oblivious curtains over Kings,
> Their sumptuous monuments, men know them not,
> Their names without a Record are forgot.
> Their parts, their ports, their pomp's all laid in th' dust
> Nor wit nor gold, nor buildings scape time's rust;
> But he whose name is grav'd in the white stone
> Shall last and shine when all of these are gone.

From such loftier strains as these, Anne Bradstreet could turn to domestic themes and the burning of her house, love for her children and, most of all, for her admirable husband. Beginning in Massachusetts as one of the chosen Assistants in the government, Simon Bradstreet served the Colony in successive posts of responsibility, rising, after her death and his second marriage, and before his death at ninety-four, to the dignity of Deputy Governor and Governor. Whatever he may have been to the state he was all in all to that Tenth Muse, his wife. Her short poem beginning:

> If ever two were one, then surely we,
> If ever man were loved by wife, then thee;

and ending:

> Then while we live, in love let's so persever,
> That when we live no more, we may live ever,

speaks timelessly for conjugal happiness. There are, besides, three letters in verse to her husband, "absent upon Publick employment." The third of these has a special seventeenth-century flavor through her likening herself to a "loving Hind (that Hartless) wants her Deer," to "the pensive Dove" that moans the absence of her mate, even to "the loving Mullet, that true fish," and, with these lines, as if of Jacobean conceit:

> Return my Dear, my joy, my only Love
> Unto thy Hinde, thy Mullet, and thy Dove,
> Who neither joyes in pasture, house, nor streams,
> The substance gone, O me, these are but dreams,
> Together at one Tree, oh let us brouze
> And like two Turtles, roost within one house,
> And like the Mullets in one River glide,
> Let's still remain but one, till death divide.

> *Thy loving Love and Dearest Dear,*
> *At home, abroad, and everywhere.*
>   A. B.

Anne Bradstreet was not the first, or the last, of poets needing to be stripped of some excess poetical baggage. In fact she had a good deal of it, but there is a residue which, quite apart from the unique circumstances of its origin, should not be permitted to perish. It was long before any other woman took such a place as hers among the poets of America. Her poetical descendants appeared sooner among the men. Of her direct descendants after the flesh, William Ellery Channing and Oliver Wendell Holmes may be named, exemplars of as distant a removal from the rooted puritanism of Anne Bradstreet as one may imagine. Yet early and late they were all New Englanders who thought for themselves.

John Brown House — Providence, Rhode Island

V

John Brown of Providence

IT IS bewildering to think how many John Browns there must have been — how many there must still be — in the world. John Brown of Ossawatomie and John Brown of Queen Victorian fame spring instantly, out of large spaces, to mind. Out of a smaller space, the smallest of all among these United States, springs John Brown of Providence. From 1787 till 1803, the last sixteen years of his life, he lived in a house of a beauty unsurpassed by any house of its period in America. If the pictures of it do not substantiate this claim, it remains only for the curious to go and look at it for themselves. This can be the more readily done since the John Brown House is now the home, semipublic, of the Rhode Island Historical Society.

The legendary boy who balked at the study of early American history because it was "all cluttered up with Adamses" would feel a corresponding grievance if he should concentrate on the history of Rhode Island, which he would find "all cluttered up" with Browns. It began as early as 1638 when Chad Brown, of like mind with Roger Williams, followed him from Salem to Rhode Island, and took an important part in the planting and growth of the

Providence settlement. In the fifth generation of descent from Chad Brown four brothers, Nicholas, Joseph, John, and Moses — named here in the order of their birth — flourished, severally and collectively, through the latter half of the eighteenth century and the earlier years of the nineteenth, to an extent quite extraordinary for any period or region. Let them be dubbed, as they have been, "John and Jo, Nick and Mo," their importance stands four-square and unimpaired.

Their interests were various, yet with a certain unity. Commerce, domestic and foreign, manufacture, legislation, patriotic effort, philanthropy, furtherance of school and college, though themselves without formal education, creators — with one brother as designer — of beautiful houses and public buildings — through these interests their large fortunes were amassed and generously dispersed. A Brown saga like that of the Forsytes would particularize their successive partnerships in business, their united and separate contributions to the life of their time and place. In the present space it is possible to consider only one of them — John Brown, whose house, here represented in pictures, was his fitting habitation.

He was born in Providence, January 27, 1736, and lived until September 29, 1803. His father, James Brown, had for wife Hope Power, whose surname survives in the name of the street on which her son's great house may now be seen, even as her Christian name of Hope, the single

West Façade — John Brown House

Parlor — John Brown House

word of the Rhode Island state motto, marked her as a Rhode Islander. Power Street runs into Benefit, so called because it was laid out for the benefit of the crowded South Main Street below it. Parallel to Power runs Benevolent Street, so designated because the Benevolent Congregational Society built a church at the corner of Benefit Street. These names are in keeping with the name of Providence itself, and seem to preserve the Christian simplicities of Roger Williams and Chad Brown.

When John Brown was thirteen years old he wrote in his "Cyphering Book," filled with mathematical rules and calculations, and dated January 27th, 1749/50, the words "John Brown the Cleverest boy in Providence Town." The word *clever* had a more inclusive meaning then than it has today, and the copper-plate script of the young cypherer suggested a scrupulosity well beyond the cleverness of our own day. His schooling may have taught him well to write and to figure. To judge from his letters it never taught him to spell, but it did nothing to curb his unusual energies. Through his early years in business, he served with his brothers in the general mercantile house of Nicholas Brown and Company. About 1770 he left it to engage in business on his own account. His brothers were more conservative than he, and after a mutiny and plague on one of their few slave ships in 1764–1765, they abandoned the "triangular" voyaging in which they were never so deeply involved as their Newport and Bristol contemporaries. John Brown, more daring, went on with it, as only one of his profitable activities.

It was proper to one who has been well defined as "an Elizabethan merchant-adventurer in a new setting" that his physical presence should have been impressive. Of medium height, but of substantial weight, it could have been no meager man who carried the walking stick and wore the pink and white striped waistcoat and the white silk stockings to be seen at the Rhode Island Historical Society. Whatever his height may have been, his breadth is said to have required the whole of a chaise seat made for two. It is further of record that when he drove abroad a small grandson perched in a stool between his knees.

Of all the spirited episodes of his life none was livelier than that in which he took a leading part — an action defined by a historian of Rhode Island, Irving B. Richman, as "the first bold, overt, organized stroke of the Revolution." In June of 1772 a British armed schooner, the *Gaspee*, pursued an American vessel, defying trade regulations at Newport, up Narragansett Bay into the Providence River. Here, led into shallow waters by the Yankee sloop she was pursuing, she ran aground. The captain of the vessel that so misled her soon reached Providence, and reported the affair direct to John Brown. Eight longboats belonging to him were promptly manned by citizens of the first repute, and rowed, with muffled oars, down the river by night. According to legend, another boatload of men from Bristol arrived upon the scene. Then the *Gaspee* was boarded and set on fire. The British authorities tried to pin the chief blame for this deed of defiance upon John Brown, and to arrest him. It is said that for many ensuing months he never slept for two successive nights in the same house, but moved from one to another of his several country seats within driving distance from Providence.

A narrower escape from British authority occurred three years later. In April of 1775, just before Lexington, Captain Wallace of the British frigate *Rose*, patrolling Narragansett Bay, seized him on a vessel of his own, on which he was carrying flour to Providence without the proper British clearance from Newport to Providence. The *Gaspee* affair had not been forgotten, and Brown was naturally regarded as a prize capture. On the vessel that had seized his own, he was transported — reputedly in irons — round Cape Cod to face the British Admiral Graves in Boston. Powerful friends in Providence and especially his brother Moses, who had recently turned Quaker, made such strong representations on his behalf that the Admiral was constrained to set him free. "A humbling stroke," wrote Ezra Stiles in his diary, "to the Tories!" John Brown's agreement to cultivate amicable relations with British officials did not prevent his instituting a suit for damages against the naval commander in Newport who had authorized his seizure. The brotherly reproof for this action from Moses Brown revealed the peaceable Quaker spirit which John could never have attained.

The fighting spirit of John Brown found full play when the Revolutionary War was in actual progress. At his shipyards he built vessels for the government. "Hope Furnace," a family enterprise, turned out cannon for the army. John Brown did not escape reproof from Governor William Greene for living in luxury while others were enduring hardships, and there were malignant whispers that some of the funds designed for government ships were diverted to the building of privateers. Yet his public services were recognized, like those of all his brothers, by election to the Rhode Island General Assembly and, three times, to the Congress of the new United States in which, to be sure, he served only after his third election. What was perhaps more important was his powerful influence in furthering the adoption, however tardy, of the Constitution by Rhode Island.

There was one action, in which all four brothers joined, that has borne perennial fruit. The College of Rhode Island, opened at Warren in 1764, was moved, largely through their efforts, to Providence, where John Brown in 1770 laid the cornerstone of University Hall on ground that had belonged to his ancestor Chad Brown. It was but natural for the college to change its name to Brown University. John Brown was its treasurer for twenty years. Its enrichments through later generations of the Brown family have been many, of which the John Carter Brown Library is one of the most notable. The admirable Moses Brown School in Providence is another monument to the family's concern for education. Would Providence be what it is today had not its merchants and manufacturers rubbed elbows for the better part of two centuries with scholars?

Had book learning played a larger part in John Brown's equipment he would hardly have written as he did in 1782 to a son visiting in Philadelphia, who might "Incline to Form a Lasting Connection with a Young Lady. . . . I have to Begg, Beceash and Intreat that it be in the best Family." If her parents would settle Twenty Thousand Pounds upon her he would double this amount. "But *above all* let her be of a virtuous Carrector, and an agreeable Disposition, a Calm and Unruffled Temper, tho Spritely and Agreeable." No bad counsel of worldly wisdom to an unmarried youth — with this addendum a few months later, when the father had reason to fear that a Young Lady not quite so young as his son might be under consideration: "A Lady 4 or 5 years older than Yourself will probably be Wurn out & as Round Backt as a Monkey by the time you are Middle Aged or in the Prime of Life. Depend upon it I will never give my Consent for you to Marry any Lady in the Universe that is older than yourself, but any years Under from One to Ten years, I shall not be Difficult."

WHO LIVED HERE?

The welfare of family, town, state, and country did not set the bounds of John Brown's activities. In 1787 he sent his ship the *General Washington* to the Far East, the first Providence vessel to enter the China trade, close on the heels of the first East Indiamen from Salem. The large profits from this voyage gave incentive to all the Providence China trade that followed. One of John Brown's daughters married the son Charles of a gigantic German, Carl Friedrich Herreschoff, one of Frederick the Great's Prussian Guards, and from him the boat-building Herreshoffs of Bristol were descended, masters of the sea on terms quite other than those of their ship-building ancestor.

It was in this same year of 1787 that John Brown's great house was built, on designs believed to have been made by his brother Joseph, who died shortly before its erection. Other objects of architectural pride in Providence, notably the First Baptist Church, are traced more or less directly to this ingenious brother, whose scientific bent accounted for his election to the American Academy of Arts and Sciences.*

* Joseph Brown built for himself the house with the waving roof line, now numbered 55 South Main Street, in which the Brown business affairs are now conducted. For some years it was the home of the Providence National Bank, of which John Brown was the first president. In the present building of that bank, with entrances on both Westminster and Weybosset Streets, five large murals of historic Providence scenes, inevitably representing members of the Brown family, were painted by R. H. Ives Gammell, a descendant of Nicholas Brown.

JOHN BROWN

When John Brown's house had been standing only two years Mrs. John Adams, stopping over in Providence on her way from Braintree, Massachusetts, to New York, visited it, and writing to her sister, Mrs. Cranch, described it as "one of the grandest I have ever seen in this country. Everything in and about it wore the marks of magnificence and taste." More than twenty persons were hastily summoned to meet her at dinner — "an elegant entertainment upon a service of plate." Her son, John Quincy Adams, seeing its exterior a few months later, described it as "the most magnificent and elegant private mansion that I have ever seen on this continent." Even before the wife of our first Vice-President and her son saw the house, President Washington himself visited it long enough to enjoy a glass of John Brown's punch.

Except for the relatively brief period of its ownership and occupancy by the late Marsden J. Perry, it remained in the possession of members of the Brown family, to which it returned when it was acquired in 1936 by Mr. John Nicholas Brown, a descendant of John's brother Nicholas, and presented by him later to the Rhode Island Historical Society.

Of the four Brown brothers, all men of high value to their community, John may be said to have cut the largest dash. His life ended when the nineteenth century was beginning. As the twentieth enters its second half his mansion stands as a rarely impressive personal monument.

Nor is that by any means all. This house, like nearly every other among the thirteen under consideration here, has been converted from private to public or semipublic uses. More and more, as time goes on, the great houses of earlier days are proving themselves beyond the needs, or resources, of their natural inheritors. Indeed it is becoming a part of what is known as the democratic process for the mansions of the few to be turned into the resorts of the many. The builders may not always have builded better than they knew, but certainly often they have achieved purposes which they could not possibly have imagined.

Emily Dickinson House — Amherst, Massachusetts

VI

Emily Dickinson: Enigma*

NO POSSESSOR of "that one talent which is death to hide" tried harder to hide it, and with less success in the end, than Emily Dickinson. If the talent be great, this effort can rarely succeed. In her case the effort did succeed through her lifetime of fifty-six years. Her familiar poem beginning "I'm nobody! Who are you?" continued:

> How dreary to be somebody!
> How public, like a frog,
> To tell your name the livelong day
> To an admiring bog!

In another poem she wrote:

> I never spoke unless addressed,
> And then 'twas brief and low.
> I could not bear to live aloud
> The racket shamed me so.

Over against these demands for complete privacy there are the lines used to introduce her collected poems, beginning:

* An impairment of vision when about half of this book was written brought to the author's aid, in the assembling of material for this and other chapters, the generous services of Mrs. Walter Muir Whitehill. For this help a warm gratitude must be expressed.

WHO LIVED HERE?

This is my letter to the world,
That never wrote to me.

and ending, "Judge tenderly of me!" — surely an admission that some notice from "the world" was more than half expected. Living in seclusion, did she really expect her poetry to remain as hidden as she kept herself? This is but one question in a large enigma.

The house in which she was born, lived, and died at Amherst, Massachusetts, is still to be seen and pictured. What of the poet who lived in it? For any purpose of portrayal she was as elusive as the butterflies she liked to write about. She was born December 10, 1830. The house was built in 1813 by her grandfather, Samuel Fowler Dickinson, graduate of Dartmouth, severe, powerful Puritan, instrumental in establishing both the Amherst Academy and its offspring, Amherst College. His son Edward, Emily's father, and his grandson, Emily's brother, both lawyers, both treasurers of Amherst College, both substantial leading citizens, maintained the family tradition of rigid New England orthodoxy.

Emily lived with her parents and her younger sister Lavinia in her grandfather's house, separated only by a hedge on the Dickinson place from the house of her brother and his wife, of special congeniality with Emily. She said that her mother did not "care for thought," and that her father was a Sunday reader of "lonely and rigorous books," who, though buying books for her,

gave warning that reading them might "joggle her mind."
To each and every one of this family circle of positive
personalities Emily was passionately devoted.

The atmosphere of her surroundings — household,
town, and college — was of that stiff religious convention best calculated to breed rebellion, and Emily was a
born rebel. After she had cut free from the Sunday habits
of her family she made bold to say, "I wish the 'faith of
our fathers' didn't wear brogans and carry blue um-
brellas," and she wrote:

> Some keep the Sabbath going to church;
> I keep it staying at home
> With a bob-o-link for a chorister,
> And an orchard for a dome.
>
> God preaches, — a noted clergyman, —
> And the sermon is never long;
> So instead of getting to heaven at last,
> I'm going all along!

Her poems show great familiarity, often a jocular familiarity, with the Bible, but beneath any surface irreverence
there was the deepest reverence for religion.

She was small of stature, with certain beauties, it is
said, especially of hair and eyes, but without beauty itself.
As a girl she gaily hoped to become the belle of Amherst
when she reached seventeen, and, gifted with capacities
of wise and witty expression beyond her fellows, won
and retained their affection. It seems to have troubled her

conscience that she could not embrace the religion of her time and place as the rest of her family did. At sixteen she was writing to an absent schoolmate, "I know not why I feel that the world holds a predominant place in my affections," and, "I feel that I have not yet made my peace with God." Her early possession of an independent spirit of her own stood revealed in a tradition of the following year, when her schooling was transferred from the Amherst Academy to the Female Seminary at South Hadley that was yet to become Mount Holyoke College. The redoubtable Mary Lyon was its head. On the day before Christmas she announced that December 25 would be observed as a day of fast, through many hours of which the girls were to sit in their rooms and meditate. The assembled school was then asked to rise in assent to this proposal. All except Emily Dickinson and her room-mate stood up. Miss Lyon then repeated her request, and, hoping to shame the two recalcitrants, asked them to rise, to be observed by all. Emily, unsupported by her room-mate, had the courage to stand alone. Thus she was enabled to join her family on Christmas Day. How comforting that may have been one questions, on learning that her father, according to her later word, "frowned upon Santa Claus and all such prowling gentlemen," of whom St. Valentine must have been another.

Shakespeare could have had no such intelligence as Emily Dickinson's in mind when he wrote, "Home-keep-

ing youth have ever homely wits." A more resolute home-
keeper than she, and one with wits of wider range, would
have been hard to find. When her schooldays were over
she kept herself more and more out of contact with all
but her family and a few beloved intimates. "Friends,"
she once declared, "are my estate." Her father's house, its
garden, birds, bees, and flowers, such children as came
her way, an understanding dog, books — when she came
to read Shakespeare she said to herself, "Why is any
other book needed?" — these, with long thoughts about
life, death, immortality, eternity, were her preoccupa-
tions, and her themes. Her immediate family and the
friends to whom her letters were often enriched by the
enclosure of bits of verse knew that she was constantly
drawing on these resources. The resulting verses were
often no more than poetic exclamations, originally jotted
on scraps of paper, grocery wrappings, backs of used en-
velopes, margins of newspapers. More carefully wrought
lines she copied, in a handwriting sometimes scarcely
legible, on sheets of paper, often with marginal notes of
alternative readings. It has been found since then that the
poet's violation of all rules of grammar and rhyme was
offset, exceptionally in the field of untrammeled verse, by
the highly individual and searching quality of what she
had to say.

Her absences from home were few and far between.
In 1864 and 1865 a serious trouble with her eyes neces-

sitated long visits to Boston for treatment by an oculist. In 1862, when her father was a member of Congress, she paid a visit, with more momentous personal consequences, to Washington and Philadelphia. In the second city she was deeply impressed by the preaching and the personality of a Presbyterian minister, the Reverend Dr. Charles Wadsworth. In a biography by Emily Dickinson's niece there are intimations of early mild "love-affairs," on which her father frowned as he did upon Santa Claus. One of them was defined as "spicy." Several sources throw light upon her far more important relations with Dr. Wadsworth, whose wife and three children placed any thought of marriage with Emily beyond question. There is every indication, however, that an intense sympathy existed between them. Her letters after his death to two brothers, his friends, leave no doubt that a large segment of her heart, if not all of it, had been given to Dr. Wadsworth. Her poems of love clearly reveal the depths of feeling of which she was capable. Among these poems are the utterances of a devoted wife — which suggests some uses to which her poetic imagination may possibly have been put.

It was a token of her zeal for privacy that she would ask others to address the letters she wrote to friends. Dr. and Mrs. J. G. Holland, for example, served as such intermediaries in her correspondence with Dr. Wadsworth. Will these letters themselves ever come to light?

After the two absences from Amherst that have been mentioned, her disappearance from common sight in her father's house and garden became more and more nearly complete. To her fellow townsmen she was known as a mysterious being, dressed always in white, pursuing a course of life as far beyond their comprehension as many of her poems would have been. The sudden death of her father, after making a vigorous speech in the Massachusetts legislature, the paralysis of her mother one year later, in 1875, and her death in 1882 deeply affected the inner life of a daughter so devoted as Emily Dickinson was to her equally beloved parents. For her there was no distinction between an inner and an outer life. It was only inner and inmost. At its core lay her expression of it, in poetry. In relation to that her sense of privacy was so great that the idea of publication was as far from her thoughts as firmament and fin, to employ her own figure, were separated. In her lifetime only two or three pieces were slipped into print — without her sanction.

A serious breakdown of health preceded her death by almost two years. On May 16, 1886, she "ceased" — that was her word describing her mother's death — and only a small circle of friends knew, as the world of letters knew not at all, that a rare and true poet had died.

Now, in the second half century since her death, she stands exalted among American poets, not merely as first in the choir of women, but, in her own distinctive performance and influence, beside Emerson, Poe, and Whitman, and of high place in the whole company of mystic poets. How did this extraordinary ascent to fame come to pass?

Certainly the April 1862 issue of the *Atlantic Monthly* had a good deal to do with it. The opening article was an unsigned "Letter to a Young Contributor." All *Atlantic* articles were then unsigned, but the secrets of authorship were open, and even as Lowell and Mrs. Stowe must have been held responsible for the "Biglow Paper" and the installment of "Agnes of Sorrento" in this issue, Thomas Wentworth Higginson was known to have written the opening article. It was a sensible article of ten pages, addressed to writers of prose rather than poetry. "Do not be made conceited," ran one of its precepts, "by obscurity, any more than by notoriety." Perhaps Emily Dickinson took these, and other words, as addressed to herself. Certainly she recognized the friendly spirit of the article and the familiarity of its author with the problems of writing. On April 12, 1862 — the *Atlantic* hardly off the press — Higginson, then a Unitarian minister in Worcester, received a letter, unsigned but enclosing a card with the name and address of Emily Dickinson. She had made bold to ask, "Are you too deeply occupied to say if my verse is alive?" and begged, "if you please, sir, to tell me what is true." The kindhearted Higginson, interested

Photo by Walter R. Fleischer. Courtesy of Harvard University News

Replica of Emily Dickinson Room now in the Houghton Library

especially in the achievements of women, made a reply which called forth a grateful response — "Thank you for your surgery; it was not so painful as I supposed" — and a long and fruitful correspondence ensued, ending only as her death, in 1886, drew near. In this period of nearly twenty-five years Higginson called twice upon her in Amherst, once recording vividly the impression she made upon him. Throughout the correspondence Emily Dickinson usually signed herself "Your Scholar." If Higginson once referred to her in a letter to his sister as "my partially cracked poetess at Amherst," he must be honored for having seen from first to last that behind all the oddities of thought and expression there was indeed a poet.

It was not until five years after Emily Dickinson's death that, in 1891, her poetry became known beyond a narrowly limited circle. Her adoring sister Lavinia had, in this interval, been gathering the scattered, often illegible, little manuscripts together, and had associated with herself in the arrangement of that material an Amherst friend and neighbor, Mrs. Mabel Loomis Todd, wife of a professor of astronomy in Amherst College, and herself an astronomer. Then it was but natural, before publication, to invoke the editorial collaboration and joint sponsorship of a known figure in the world of letters, none other than Thomas Wentworth Higginson. The Houghton Mifflin firm found the Poems "too queer" for its respectable list. Roberts Brothers was more daring, and late in 1890, under the date of 1891, a small volume, edited by Higginson and Mrs. Todd, with an Introduction by Higginson and a cover stamped with an Indian pipe design by Mrs. Todd, was issued by that firm. It passed quickly into eleven editions, and was followed in 1892 by *Poems, Second Series* with the same joint editors, in 1894 by the *Letters of Emily Dickinson*, and in 1896 by *Poems, Third Series*, each edited by Mrs. Todd alone.

As one of the few surviving readers of adult books in the early nineties, I can testify to the excitement these volumes produced in and beyond my own circle. This must have surprised even my fellow-admirers who could hear behind all the defiances of conventional verse the voice of a new singer, dealing with nature, life, and death — with occasional stabs of delicious humor — after a fashion neither imitative nor imitable. The greater surprise awaited those whose ears were deaf to such notes. In the *Atlantic Monthly* Thomas Bailey Aldrich, its editor through the eighties, wrote, "Miss Dickinson's versicles have a queerness and a quaintness that has stirred a momentary curiosity in emotional bosoms. Oblivion lingers in the immediate neighborhood." The first British review to reach Amherst called the Poems a "farrago of illiterate and uneducated sentiment," and before long the London *Daily News* was saying of Emily Dickinson, "This lady dwelt remote, in an American village, a maid whom there were few to quote and very few to read."

Alas for prophecy! Alas, too, for the division of control over all the material that awaited editing and publication in 1896. Since Emily Dickinson herself, and not the conflicts of other personalities, with an exacerbating lawsuit, is here the object of prime concern, it would be superfluous to consider in any detail why it was not till 1914 that another volume of poems, *The Single Hound*, appeared, with *Further* and *Unpublished* poems and so-called *Complete Poems* to follow. For completeness one cannot yet turn to any single book. Biographies of varying merit — *This Was a Poet* (1938) by George F. Whicher, standing early and high among them — are multiplying. Emily Dickinson's niece, Mrs. Bianchi, in her *Life and Letters*, and *Emily Dickinson Face to Face*, and Mrs. Todd's daughter, Mrs. Bingham, in *Ancestors' Brocade*, have produced illuminating, if not final, books. The strange story of *Bolts of Melody*, a volume of poems published in 1945, must be told in barest outline. After the 1896 *Poems* appeared Mrs. Todd locked in a camphorwood box a mass of Emily Dickinson's manuscripts still to be considered for publication. It was not until 1929 that she permitted her daughter to open the box, with a key that set off a little tune, for the poetry box, appropriately enough, was also a music box. Mrs. Todd died in 1932, a year after she produced a new and enlarged edition of the letters. Her daughter went on with the examination and editing of the hundreds of unpublished poems found in the camphorwood box, and *Bolts of Melody* was the result. The hundreds of poems, finished and fragmentary, contained in this volume are yet to be found in any "Complete" edition.

It now appears that the study of Emily Dickinson's unique personality and poetry can be pursued under dispassionate auspices. Through private generosity a large collection of her papers — poems, diaries, and miscellany — has been placed in the Houghton Library of Harvard University. There they are deposited in a special room, furnished with the family portraits, books, and other objects among which the poet did much of her writing, and a qualified editorial board will deal with these "Papers of Emily Dickinson." Some day there should be a truly complete edition of her writing, and — who knows? — perhaps a definitive critical biography which, together, will establish for all time her pre-eminent place in American letters.

The editors must not expect to persuade posterity that Emily Dickinson was, in her multitudinous verses, by any means always at her astonishing best in the compression of great truths and beauties into a few poignant lines. The editors must not forget that "Your Scholar" was not her invariable signature in writing to Colonel Higginson. She called herself also "Your Gnome" — and Gnomes are no such manageable subjects for biography as Scholars.

VII

Christopher Gore of Gore Place

IT SEEMS a part of the eternal fitness of things when you can look at a house and at the man who built and lived in it, and find them perfectly adapted to each other. There, you say, is the very man for that house — and there is the very house for that man. You look at Gore Place in Waltham, Massachusetts, and wonder what manner of man could have made such provision for himself in a small New England town about a hundred and fifty years ago. Then you pick up the threads of the story of Christopher Gore — not all available in any one place — and you find that he was precisely the man for the house.

His American ancestors had come early to New England. He was born in Boston, September 28, 1758. At the outbreak of the Revolution his father, with others of Tory proclivities, went to Halifax. The young Christopher had entered Harvard College at thirteen, and was graduated in 1776, having formed one of the closest friendships of his life, with Rufus King of New York, of the class next below him, and in later life a leading member of the Federalist party, in which Gore also held a conspicuous place.

Serving briefly in the American army, and entering the profession of law, he advanced rapidly in its practice. Still a young man when the war was over and the new government was forming, he served in the State Convention which adopted the Constitution of the United States, and was appointed by Washington the first United States Attorney for Massachusetts. Intelligence and personal charm were already doing much to further his fortunes.

The house at Waltham was yet to come, after an important episode in his life yet to be touched upon. Both before and after that episode he was practicing law in Boston. A young man reading law in his office in 1804 was Daniel Webster, then twenty-two years old. If Gore's Federalism affected Webster's political thinking, it was in these terms that the pupil recalled his teacher, as lawyer and as man. "He is a lawyer of eminence and a deep and varied scholar. . . . He has great amenity of manners, is easy, accessible, and communicative, and, take him all in all, I could not wish a better preceptor."

It appears furthermore that Webster owed to Gore his initiation into a taste for wine. Noticing how pallid and poorly the law student looked, Gore found that he was living on corned beef, cabbage, and water. "That will never do," said Gore, and saw to it that Madeira was added to his diet. Thus Webster, in words ascribed to him, "was enabled to pursue my studies and perform my task with renewed ardor." Gore's bestowals of larger hospitalities were about to begin. The chief scene of these hospitalities was the mansion he built at Waltham on his return in 1804 from the long episode in his life passed in England as one of the commissioners charged with settling, under Jay's Treaty, the claims of American citizens for spoliation during the Revolution. His friend Rufus King was U.S. Minister to Great Britain at this time, and during a temporary absence entrusted to Gore the responsibilities of *chargé d'affaires*. His official position brought him into relations with the more privileged class in England, and its manner of life, especially on country estates, appealed to him strongly. Before leaving home he had himself acquired a considerable estate in Waltham, and had built a wooden house on it. On the first night of his sleeping in this house he had dreamed that it would be burned — and so it was, during his stay in England. It was quite natural that when he came home he should bring with him the plans for a new house, drawn by an English architect. There were plans also for planting, after the best fashions of England, and from 1804 to 1808 Gore devoted himself to establishing a country residence suited in every way to his taste. The result was a mansion that would have seemed more at home in Virginia, and still more so in England, than in New England. It was the ideal house for such a figure in the Federalist party, with its aversion from "Jeffersonian simplicity," as Gore was destined to become. The illustrations of this chapter render superfluous any words describing the house; the portrait of Gore by John Trumbull, and that of his wife, Rebecca Amory Payne, now to be seen at Gore Place, speak for the comeliness of both host and hostess.

In the words of that vivacious chronicler, John T. Morse, Jr. (still "Jr." when he died at ninety-seven), Gore was "a genuine Grandee of the Old School." Between his serving in both houses of the Massachusetts legislature and later as U.S. Senator, he was Governor of Massachusetts for the year of 1809–1810, and "liked the position so well," to employ further the words of Morse, "that he was fain to try it again. Thereupon he had his four horses harnessed to his stately coach, and made a sort of royal canvassing tour of the State. But the toilers in the fields were not favorably affected towards a candidate who went driving about in a four-in-hand, and he lost the election."

Such was the impending fate of the Federalist party. More in sympathy with England than with France, sharing with Hamilton the belief that the few were better rulers than the many, it could not long maintain its dominance in Massachusetts, or elsewhere. For Gore, with ample wealth and abundant resources of intellectual and social pleasures, the relief from public duties, when failing health caused him to resign his seat in the Senate, had its compensations. Without children of his own, he enjoyed the society of the young, and, a strong believer in physical

Gore Place — Waltham, Massachusetts

The Oval Room — Gore Place

Dining Room Mantel — Gore Place

exercise for himself, told such young friends among the undergraduates at Harvard as a son of Rufus King that if they would walk to his house in Waltham he would send them back to Cambridge by chaise. The hospitalities of Gore Place were many, and outside the house its master took much pleasure in its adornment with trees and gardens, encouraging his wife the while in her interest in the dairy. Like the Englishmen he admired he furnished the house itself with a "gentleman's library," and for a final touch of similitude enjoyed especially the reading of his Horace.

In Gore's letters to Rufus King the interests of a "grandee of the Old School," committed to the old rather than the new order for his kind, are clearly reflected. One letter relating to his health discloses his resort to rubbings by a Rhode Island blacksmith, though with little faith that it would cure his rheumatism. Of the various curatives used by this practitioner one was "a decoction of cherry tree and white oak bark," another a "liquor composed of New England rum and salt peter dissolved therein, and strong vinegar" — a treatment from which a conservative of our time would shrink!

For self-treatment he stuck to his daily walks about his place, and to the Waltham meetinghouse on Sundays. His three-cornered beaver hat, hung over his pew in full view of the congregation, was an impressive object. Still more was the Governor himself as he walked to church, "attired in the old style, with knee breeches and silver shoe buckles." To cap it all there was his peruke, tied behind "with a ribbon at the neck," and dressed with powder.

His death at Waltham, March 1, 1829, closed a full life of more than seventy years. Besides the political positions that have been mentioned, Gore had served as both an Overseer and a Fellow of Harvard College, and as President of the Massachusetts Historical Society. His bequest of $100,000 to Harvard College was larger than any single benefaction previously received — a fact worth noting in these days of millions. The College applied it to the sorely needed building of a library, and for many years Gore Hall, the granite blend of King's College Chapel in Cambridge and the old Fitchburg Railroad Station in Boston, served an invaluable purpose. When this building was superseded by the Widener Library, Harvard was briefly without a Gore Hall, but the name was bestowed on one of the Freshman dormitories now incorporated, under the same name, in John Winthrop House. Gore Hall in Cambridge and Gore Place in Waltham may then be regarded as cousins, though not of the same generation. About twenty years ago more than two hundred volumes, chiefly of classical literature, from Gore's own library, came to the Harvard College Library from members of the King family who had inherited them.

CHRISTOPHER GORE

For more than a century following the death of Christopher Gore his Place passed through a succession of private ownerships. One family followed another, with a responsibility for preserving and enhancing its beauty. When more recently it became in turn an automobile office, a country club, and a roadhouse, disguised at one time under a coat of white paint, its future looked dim. The final prospect of its loss through a development which would have destroyed the house and covered its grounds with small dwellings led a few public-spirited citizens to form the Gore Place Society, which has brought it back to something very like its original condition and established an enduring memorial not merely of an individual man but also of an entire period.

Christopher Gore's place among the political figures of his time may have fallen short of the highest distinction, but as a man in relation to a superb house he was notably a round peg in a round hole.

VIII

Hawthorne, Emerson, and the Old Manse

NATHANIEL HAWTHORNE twice gave enduring names to well-known local habitations in America. If he had not come, newly married, to Concord, Massachusetts, and settled there in an ancient parsonage where he wrote his *Mosses from an Old Manse,* the house would never have been known as such. If he had not moved a few years later to Lenox, in the same state, and there given the name of "Tanglewood" to his immediate surroundings, another familiar designation would have been missing. At Tanglewood he stands alone in distinguished association with a place and its name. In Concord it is different, for another figure of the highest distinction in American letters, Ralph Waldo Emerson, must be placed beside him.

Emerson's identification with the old house was more hereditary than personal, though from time to time he did dwell within its walls. Indeed it was in the same study, haunted with spirits of Puritan divines, that Emerson began the writing of *Nature,* published in 1836, and Hawthorne wrote many of his "Mosses," which appeared ten years later in a book. In each instance the author was making an early announcement of what he was to become. If the Adams Mansion in Quincy stands apart from all other houses in America through the continuous notable productions of a single family, the Old Manse stands equally alone as a historic landmark of letters in that two such towering figures as Emerson and Hawthorne each lived and wrote in it.

In the few pages available here it would be impertinent — and irrelevant to the general purpose of this little book — to attempt any fresh appraisal of these two figures — truly classic figures in the American frame of literary reference. Perhaps the reader needs to be reminded that in the 1840's they were as "modern" as the latest apparitions of our own familiar decades seemed when they first appeared. And they were relatively young — Emerson only forty in 1843, and Hawthorne thirty-nine. Then brought together by an accident of time and place, each was a special product of the New England civilization out of which they grew. Unlike as they were, each made a distinctive contribution to American life as it stands revealed in written words. What they wrote may be read and reread for a continued comprehension of American meanings.

Emerson's ancestral identification with the house was complete. It was built in 1769 by his grandfather, the Reverend William Emerson, of whom it is told that in his boyhood his father charged him, when on his way to church one morning, with walking as if the earth were not good enough for him, to which he replied, in all humility, "I did not know it, Sir," an anecdote quite of that special flavor now known as Emersonian. The Concord minister both shared and stimulated the spirit of his patriotic parishioners, became a chaplain with the Revolutionary army at Ticonderoga, and died of a fever in October 1776. Already the Concord Fight at the river that skirted the Emerson parsonage had predestined its rude bridge to be known, as the shot fired there was to be heard, round the world — and this through the words of the patriot parson's grandson.

Even as William Emerson had married the daughter of his predecessor in the Concord pulpit, the Rev. Daniel Bliss, so his successor, the Rev. Ezra Ripley, married her as the Widow Emerson, already the mother of three children. So the parsonage continued the home of Emerson's grandmother, now Mrs. Ripley, and to its shelter he frequently resorted. There are few better instances of the linking of historic with domestic happenings than an entry in Emerson's Journal of 1834 to the effect that Dr. Ripley was asked at breakfast whether the cow should be driven into the battlefield. Long before Emerson's Journal saw the light of day this story must have got abroad, for in 1853 George William Curtis told it with the elaboration of naming the inquiring cow-boy Jeremiah or

Nicodemus, and reporting Dr. Ripley's order for the cow, "Into the battle-field, Nicodemus, into the battle-field!"

When Emerson's widowed mother and her boys found their circumstances too straitened to remain long in Boston after the second Reverend William Emerson died in 1811, the hospitable Ripleys took them into the parsonage for the winter of 1814–1815. Emerson himself, then only eleven years old, acquitted himself well in the Concord school. The parsonage and the town, with its ancestral ties far beyond enumeration here, were twined into the fibers of his being. He found himself again at the parsonage in 1825, and beside the fireplace in an upper room came upon a wooden panel inscribed by his father in 1780 and his brother Edward in 1824. To these he added his own inscription: "Peace to the soul of the blessed dead, honor to the ambition of the living."

After nearly ten years he returned to the parsonage, in 1834, rather as a resident than a mere visitor. Much had befallen him meanwhile: marriage with his first wife, her death, and his own first visit to Europe. On his return in 1833 he had no settled place of abode until he moved with his mother from Newton, packing her few household possessions and his own on a cart secured for them by his step-grandfather, Ezra Ripley, under whose roof he now lived for a year. It was a busy year, with an important Concord historical address to prepare and deliver, and ending with his second marriage in September to Lydia Jackson of Plymouth — misnamed Lydia by her parents, he said, for her name was really Lydian. He had "dodged the doom of building" by acquiring a house of his own in Concord in which he was to live for the rest of his days. But in an upper chamber of the old parsonage he began putting into final form his first book, *Nature,* of which he had been thinking even on shipboard as he returned from Europe, noting in his Journal: "I like my book about Nature, and only wish I knew where and how I ought to live." Thus the Old Manse, a milestone book, and the man for whom it marked a first long step into his total greatness of thinking and writing, were brought into close conjunction.

Between Hawthorne and the Old Manse there was no such ancestral and cerebral relation. It was much more a matter of romance, for it was to this very house that Hawthorne came immediately upon his marriage in 1842 with Sophia Peabody. In it he passed his first three years of married life, and gave his latest biographer, Professor Randall Stewart, full occasion to declare that "the life of the newly married pair at the Old Manse is the classic of American marital idyls."

It may well be that this parsonage was never called a manse before Hawthorne entered it. If he had not called it the Old Manse in the essay which stood first in his second book of sketches, *Mosses from an Old Manse* (1846),

The Old Manse — Concord, Massachusetts

Small Parlor — The Old Manse

Dining Room in the Old Manse — Concord, Massachusetts

the name could hardly have come into common use. Hawthorne's own association with the house bore a close relation with his sojourn at Brook Farm immediately preceding his marriage. He had advanced $1000 for the support of that enterprise, and on deciding to quit it, hoped to arrange for the return of this sum from George Ripley, a kinsman of Ezra Ripley, and head of the Brook Farm experiment. Apparently Hawthorne's occupancy of the Manse had something to do with this transaction, in which it is not clear either that Hawthorne recovered his advance or that he was able finally to keep up with expected payments of rent. Such questions of dollars and cents, however, were so foreign to the atmosphere in which his writing enveloped the house that the answers need not be sought too diligently.

Yet one financial point may well be touched upon. This was Hawthorne's provision for some assurance of income to meet the demands of matrimony. Shortly before entering upon it he visited Albany and made arrangements with the editor of the *Democratic Review*, a popular periodical which paid its contributors at the pitiful rates then prevailing, for the series of sketches that eventually filled many pages of his *Mosses*.

It is in the opening essay, "The Old Manse," in this book that one finds a description of the house, to which Hawthorne and his wife came as a new Adam and Eve to a new Paradise. The little study in which he worked, the very room on which Emerson had worked on his *Nature*, surrounded by the depressing portrait-prints which the Hawthornes removed from its walls, the "Saint's Chamber" under the rough-hewn rafters of the upper story, the small-paned windows, the views from within, the Lethean river, hardly saying which way it flowed, the garden and the vegetables over which Hawthorne worked more happily than over the dung heaps of Brook Farm, the orchard with its symbolically gnarled apple trees — all these and other aspects of the place challenged his characteristic observation. Even when he repeats a grisly, dubious story told him by Lowell about a Concord boy chopping wood for Emerson's grandfather on the day of the Concord Fight, and on his way to look at it, swinging his axe into the head of a wounded British soldier, it is unmistakably Hawthorne who caps the story by saying, "Oftentimes, as an intellectual and moral exercise, I have sought to follow that poor youth through his subsequent career, and observe how his soul was tortured by the blood stain."

When Hawthorne left the Old Manse in 1845 it was for good, though he returned in later years to live in Concord. Emerson left it to marry and settled elsewhere in the town, but often visited his Ripley relatives in the Old Manse — the Reverend Ezra's son, the Reverend Samuel, and his prodigiously learned wife — and there he and his family were received as refugees when his own house was burned. Here our direct concern is with Hawthorne's three years in the Manse and the relations between him and Emerson while he was there.

What the two men thought about each other may be learned, with some precision, in their respective writings, especially their journals. They met not infrequently, but never, as one may clearly infer, with complete sympathy. They took a two days' walking trip together, and Hawthorne could not remember afterwards just what they said to each other. Emerson did better, alluding to "excellent spirits" and "much conversation," though based largely on their being "both old collectors who had never had opportunity before to show each other our cabinets." Subsequent meetings led only to disappointment on Emerson's part in so far as any real getting together was concerned. However conversational Hawthorne may have been when they walked together for two days, his reputation for taciturnity in society is confirmed by Curtis's report of an "aesthetic tea" at Emerson's house where Hawthorne held so resolute a silence that on his departure Emerson remarked, "Hawthorne rides well his horse of the night."

Hawthorne might write in his Journal, "Mr. Emerson came with a sunbeam in his face; and we had as good a talk as I ever remember experiencing with him." On the other hand he could write in his "Old Manse" sketch that although once he might have asked of this prophet to

solve him the riddle of the universe, "Now, being happy"
— to use his very words — "I felt as if there were no question to be put, and therefore admired Emerson as a poet
of deep beauty and austere tenderness, but sought nothing
of him as a philosopher." Elsewhere, Emerson appears to
him as "the mystic, stretching his hand out of cloud-land,
in vain search for something real." And still again he sees
him as "that everlasting rejector of all that is, and seeker
for he knows not what."

Though Emerson counted Hawthorne before he came
to the Old Manse among those who "if added to our present kings and queens, would make a rare, an unrivalled
company," he could not fit him into the Concord pattern
neatly enough to prevent his noting in his Journal that,
"Alcott and he together would make a man." (What
would either Hawthorne or Alcott have said to this?)
In Hawthorne's writing Emerson found less than in the
man himself, even though their personal relation was
never so unreserved as he would have had it. "Nathaniel
Hawthorne's reputation as a writer," he wrote in his Journal, "is a very pleasing fact, because his writing is not
good for anything, and this *is* a tribute to the man." Was
it the frankness and intimacy with which Hawthorne described his own and his wife's happiness in the Old Manse
which led Emerson to write as he did in 1846, the year in
which the *Mosses* appeared as a book? "Hawthorne," in
Emerson's view, "invites his readers too much into his

study and opens the process before them, as if the confectioner should say to his customers, 'Now, let us make the cake.' "

Concerning others than Emerson in Concord Hawthorne expressed himself with candor. He needed not to go far beyond the Old Manse "before meeting with stranger moral shapes of men than might have been encountered elsewhere in a circuit of a thousand miles." He called them "hobgoblins of flesh and blood," drawn to Concord by the wide-spreading influence of Emerson. The native product for whom he cared most was Thoreau — "ugly as sin," he called him, but with an ugliness "of an honest and agreeable fashion." They rowed, swam, and talked together on the Concord River and Walden — clearly congenial spirits. A less considerable member of Emerson's circle got hardly more from Hawthorne than the characterization, "A gnome yclept Ellery Channing," whose verses seemed to himself "too sacred to be sold for money." Of the remarkable women of Concord, Elizabeth Hoar was, for Hawthorne, "much more at home among spirits than among fleshly bodies." Of Emerson's extraordinary Aunt Mary Moody Emerson, whose maxims, such as "Always do what you are afraid to do," made deep impressions upon her nephew in youth, one could only wish to learn that Hawthorne was living at the Manse when this strange lady rode to it "sidewise on a man's saddle," to borrow the description of her nephew, "arrayed in her dimity shroud, which, tired of waiting for death, she used as a day-gown, and over it, on this occasion, threw a scarlet shawl." Hawthorne should have been standing between the stone gateposts of the Manse to welcome her.

Of feminine society, whether strange or conventional, Hawthorne had no need at the time. It was a honeymoon period of three years. His adored and adoring bride, proud of everything he did, rejoicing equally in the grace of his skating on the frozen Concord River, in his performance of household and garden chores, and in his writing, made the new Eden of the Old Manse Paradise enow for Hawthorne. To crown it all, it was in this period that their first child, their daughter Una, was born. When the Hawthornes moved to Salem, late in 1845, the Reverend Samuel Ripley and his family occupied the Old Manse.

For the better part of a century the Manse had housed especially the austerities of mind, spirit, and old age. Now for three years it had become the home of art, imagination, and young life. For the greater part of another century the house remained in the hands to which Hawthorne relinquished it — those of the Ripley family, with the astonishing Mrs. Samuel Ripley, daughter of one Gamaliel Bradford, and brought to life in the "psychograph" of another. She was a Concordian after Emerson's own heart, and one whom Hawthorne might have studied as a rare product of the old New England that was his peculiar province. Without and within the house itself kept the special quality that matched its history. The essence of it all counted more than its appearance.

When the last representative of the Ripley family to live in it, though only as a summer residence, was working one day in the garden where Hawthorne used to work, he heard "the Voice" of a sight-seeing bus that was passing declare: "Here is the celebrated Old Manse. In the hands of its present owners it has fallen into complete decay." If that had been true — which it was not — the acquisition of the Manse in 1939 by the Trustees of Public Reservations in Massachusetts would have been even more desirable than it is. The face of weathered wood may some day be lifted. Grass and shrubs through the years to come may be neatly trimmed. This matters less than that the ancient parsonage, notably inhabited through nearly two hundred years, is now assured continuance. And it will continue to be haunted by memorable spirits.

IX

Sarah Orne Jewett, of the Pointed Firs Country

EVERYBODY knows what Sir Walter Scott wrote when he had been reading, "for the third time at least, Miss Austen's very finely written novel of Pride and Prejudice." Her talent in her own field seemed to him the most wonderful he ever met with. "The Big Bow-wow strain," he went on to declare, "I can do myself like any now going; but the exquisite touch, which renders commonplace things and characters interesting, from the truth of the description and the sentiment, is beyond me."

An American counterpart of Sir Walter, were there any such, might have expressed himself in like manner about Sarah Orne Jewett. No one of her three novels is comparable with any of Jane Austen's immortal six. Her units of production — short stories or related sketches brought together in a single book — were smaller than Miss Austen's units; her characters were in general far simpler folk than the county gentry of England, but in exquisite touch, in mastery of the commonplace, the analogy between the two writers is little short of perfect.

Sarah Orne Jewett lived longer than Jane Austen —

Sarah Orne Jewett House — South Berwick, Maine

Central Hallway — Sarah Orne Jewett House

Miss Jewett's Own Room
West Parlor — Sarah Orne Jewett House

sixty years against only forty-two. Her perpetual industry as a writer, from girlhood to the end of her days, produced results in the bare terms of pages of print considerably exceeding those of Jane Austen. For purposes of the comparison I have suggested, Miss Jewett's novels and a number of her short stories hardly need to be considered. In Miss Austen's small output there were fewer departures from her best. It was with Miss Jewett's best in mind that Willa Cather, whose standards manifested in her own writing give special weight to her words, declared as late as 1925, "If I were asked to name three American books which have the possibility of a long, long life, I should say at once: *The Scarlet Letter, Huckleberry Finn,* and *The Country of the Pointed Firs.* I think of no others that confront time and change so serenely. The last book seems to me fairly to shine with reflection of its long joyous future." And Miss Cather proceeds to picture the pleasure and sense of rich discovery with which "the young student of American literature in far distant years to come will take up this book and say, 'A masterpiece!' as proudly as if he himself had made it."

The Country of the Pointed Firs is clearly Miss Jewett's own masterpiece. From what did the excellence — a quality by no means limited to this single book — proceed? The rectory at Steventon and the Jewett house at South Berwick, Maine, had this in common — that each represented in the community to which it belonged the local best in respect of the atmosphere and influences which go to the nourishing of mind and spirit. The Jewett house — in which Miss Jewett was born (September 3, 1849), in which she lived and died — built about 1750 in sound colonial style, was acquired by her grandfather, prosperous owner and builder of ships sailing to the West Indies and the Mediterranean from their home port of South Berwick — *Barvik* in the older generation's speech of Miss Jewett's girlhood. Even as the ships sailed up and down the few miles of the Piscataqua above the coastal town of Portsmouth, so their timber and masts floated down that river from the woodlands to the shipyards of their common owner. To his house came his captains reporting on their voyages, and to his granddaughter he seemed "a citizen of the whole geography." Here she was beginning to acquire the wisdom which led her to say in later years, "You must know the whole world before you know the village."

From her father she learned most of all. His studious tastes led him not into business but to Bowdoin College, where he cultivated that love of good books which caused him to furnish the shelves of the Jewett house with leather-bound copies of the English classics. His profession became that of a physician — a Country Doctor such as his daughter depicted in her novel of that name. Sarah Jewett's delicate health caused many interruptions in her schooling at the South Berwick Academy. Fortunately the books at home and the drives about the country with her father as he visited his patients more than made up for any loss of scholastic training. As father and daughter drove from fishermen's houses along the shore to inland farms, he told her many stories of his patients, and while he was indoors with them she was making acquaintances with the up-and-about, adding directly to her own local lore. Was it at this time that the nickname of "Pinny," used in the "Little language" of her correspondence with her beloved Mrs. Fields, was bestowed, as she once wrote, "because she was so straight and thin and her head no bigger than a pin's"?

She was only about thirteen when she read Harriet Beecher Stowe's *Pearl of Orr's Island*, and began to see the life about her on a printed page. Before long she was making her own experiments in writing, less in prose than in verse, which she found the easier medium. At nineteen she ventured to offer her modest wares to editors, and soon after turning twenty she saw two of her stories in print — "Mr. Bruce" in the *Atlantic Monthly* for December 1869, and "The Shipwrecked Buttons" (not even remotely related to the *Tender Buttons* of Gertrude Stein) in the juvenile *Riverside Magazine* for January 1870. Miss Jewett — or was it possibly Mrs. Fields? — used to tell a story of an English lady in sadly straitened circumstances who was driven to the necessity of selling sprats on the streets of London. Placing herself in the most obscure spot she could find, she kept saying in a feeble voice, "Sprats, sprats. I hope nobody will hear me!" At first Sarah Jewett had no wish to be heard in her proper person, and used the pseudonym of Alice Eliot. The disguise could not long be maintained, and the editorial relations with Horace E. Scudder of the *Riverside*, and James T. Fields and William D. Howells of the *Atlantic* soon led into enduring friendships.

Miss Jewett was such a reader of books — and, incidentally, of few but the best — that she once wrote to Mrs. Fields: "I feel as if I had been over-eating with my head." The reading habit began early, with the consequence that, small-town girl as she was, the horizon of her mind was anything but local. When her acquaintance in the world of letters began to grow and her visits to Boston and other places became more frequent, she was found to be an accomplished young woman of no inconsiderable beauty and charm. Perhaps a little deliberately, and half humorously, she held, early and late, to the speech and bearing suggestive of a country rather than a city background. Certainly she gave no impression of taking herself too seriously. It was delightful to hear only the other day of her once saying, "Most of us are not so large as our bodies. I come up only to my own shoulder."

Her editorial and personal association with the *Atlantic Monthly*, begun early and long continued, was her closest relationship of its kind. Her writings became welcome in a number of other periodicals, but the *Atlantic* connection, so to call it, had a vital bearing on the whole second half of her life. James T. Fields, of the firm which published the magazine, and its second editor — between Lowell and Howells — died in 1881. Through the preceding decade Sarah Jewett had formed a friendship with him and his gifted and beautiful wife, Annie Fields, fifteen years her senior. In 1877 the publication of *Deephaven* had won for Miss Jewett, then twenty-eight years old, a wide recognition. The fact that the book, picturing a Maine coast village in the early days of contact between "natives" and summer visitors, brought together a number of sketches first printed in the *Atlantic* gave it a special interest to Fields and his wife. And what a rare and charming person was its author!

Now Sarah Jewett once wrote to a friend that she needed a wife more than a husband. In so far as one can tell, the idea of acquiring a husband never occurred to her. The daughter of the Country Doctor in her so-named novel is represented as a young woman who put aside all thought of love and marriage in favor of becoming herself a doctor — a type of those girls who regard the following of their own bent as more important than any other course. It may not be fantastic to believe that the Country Doctor's daughter of fiction and of fact had this feeling in common. Miss Jewett's domestic affections were strong. Besides her father and mother there were two sisters to whom she was devotedly attached. Her capacity for friendship was also large, and at the death of Fields it was but natural that the close friendship she had formed with his childless wife, now left alone, should become closer still. From 1881 till Miss Jewett's death in 1909 she found in Mrs. Fields not so much that wife who was preferable to a husband as a beloved and most sympathetic older sister and friend. The two women thus became, and ever remained, as nearly inseparable as the distance between South Berwick and Boston, or the nearby Manchester, would permit. The long winter and summer visits paid to the older by the younger woman provided the companionship each enjoyed, and doubled the charm of the hospitality dispensed by Mrs. Fields in that Charles Street house of hers in which for many years she maintained a close American approach to the salons of the older world. Willa Cather found that "the unique charm of Mrs. Fields's house was not that it was a place where one could hear about the past, but that it was a place where the past lived on." Here was nothing of what has been called "swimming in the seductive sea of Christian names." Here, rather, there was talk of Mr. Dickens, Mr. Browning, Mr. Emerson, Mr. Hawthorne, and the like, as if they had only just left the room.

It was to this shrine of associations with the Flowering and Indian Summer of New England that, in my twenties as a beginning editor and writer, I was brought by my slightly older friend, Charles Townsend Copeland, then Boston journalist yet to become famed at Harvard as "Copey," to make my first bow to Mrs. Fields and Miss Jewett. This was before *The Country of the Pointed Firs* was published, but I remember well Copeland's enthusiasm for Miss Jewett's story "The White Heron," and his admirable reading of that beautiful example of her art. What came ultimately of my first visit to the long-vanished 148 Charles Street may be seen in my book, *Memories of a Hostess*, drawn from the journals of Mrs. Fields, and, less observably, in a friendship with Miss Jewett which has demanded something in the writing of these pages that could not possibly have sprung from our cordial relations through the editorial offices of the *Youth's Companion* and the *Atlantic Monthly*.

Soon after the death of Fields his widow and Miss Jewett made their close friendship closer still by paying a long visit to Europe together. Whittier saw them off with a poem, "Godspeed," in which they were characterized in these lines:

> . . . Love follows her in whom
> All graces and sweet charities unite
> The old Greek beauty set in holier light,
> And her for whom New England's byways bloom,
> Who walks among us welcome as the spring,
> Calling up blossoms where her light feet stray.

Nearly ten years later they went to Europe again. Each time they visited Tennyson, to Miss Jewett the greatest of men, and met with all manner of congenial spirits from Christina Rossetti to George DuMaurier, the Provençal poet, Mistral, and their old friend and enthusiast for Miss Jewett's writings, Henry James. In Paris there was Madame Blanc ("Th. Bentzon") whose admiration for Miss Jewett's writings led to some translation of them for the *Revue des Deux Mondes*. When *The Tory Lover*, the last and most ambitious of Miss Jewett's three less than satisfying novels, appeared in another French periodical as *Le Roman d'un Royaliste*, an introductory note signed "Th. Bentzon" must have been dictated and not verified in type, for it described the author as *un écrivain célèbre aux États Unis, Miss Sarah Juvelt*. In the signature at the end of the *Roman* the name *Jewett* came into its own, for some rescue of international fame. This was rendered more secure by the publication of other translated writings of hers in a book of their own. Of this she wrote to the Thomas Bailey Aldriches that Madame Blanc had sent to her "a volume of S. O. J. all in French, which caused such pride of heart that no further remarks are ventured on the subject."

It is only in Miss Jewett's letters, not in any of her fiction, that reflections of her life in the world of letters and society are to be found. From this world she resorted gladly to South Berwick, and, except for writing "on

Mantel in East Parlor — Sarah Orne Jewett House

order" a volume, *The Normans*, for a historical series, she dealt again and again, in her short stories and in her first and second novels, *The Country Doctor* and *Marsh Island*, with the scenes and people of her lifelong association. Now and then she introduced Irish and French-Canadian characters into her Maine surroundings, but it is noticeable that she never caught their speech in the sure net which held the talk of her own Down-Easters. She flourished in the heyday of dialect stories, when the Tennessean "hit air" for "it is" was only one of many regional locutions with which a reader had to familiarize himself. In this time she stood apart through her sparing use of phonetic spelling, her skill in suggesting the sound of speech by a few exact renderings, and by the quiet turning of characteristic expressions. There was no need of underscoring anything she wrote. Lowell summed it up admirably in his dictum: "Above all she is discreet in dialect, using it for flavor but not, as is the wont of many, so oppressively as to suggest garlic."

Taking a spray of the fragrant, retiring, exquisite trailing arbutus as a symbol of New England virtue, the late Charles Miner Thompson — if I may paraphrase a few of his admirable words — offered it also as a symbol of Miss Jewett and her modest and delightful art. That art may be studied in a number of successive books.

An artist in any field is entitled to judgment in the light of the best example of his art. After all that has been said, and cited, in praise of Miss Jewett as a writer, *The Country of the Pointed Firs* may confidently be named as the single volume in which her special qualities are most clearly concentrated, and by this book her admirers, of whom I am emphatically one, would like best to have her place in American fiction determined. It is a place not loudly but quietly claimed by the perfection with which she has shown forth a departed phase of American life. A sympathetic city visitor, a young woman, comes one summer to a village on the Maine coast. It is before the days of put-putting motorboats and honking Ford cars, when such small craft as sailing dories skirt the shore and schooners are passing up and down at sea, when visits to coastal and inland farms are paid in open wagons, when the humor and pathos in the thinking and speaking of mariners and farmers retain their undiluted Down-East flavor. It was the work of an artist of the first order to deal with this material after a fashion which presented the local and limited in terms of the universal. Such an artist was Sarah Orne Jewett.

Throughout her life her work had been hampered by delicate health. Several years before her death she met with a serious accident through the overturning of a carriage and a fall that injured both head and spine. Till her death, June 24, 1909, her life became largely that of an invalid, relieved by occasional visits to Boston, and the interludes of brief summer cruises on the sailing-yachts of friends, and a winter cruise in the Caribbean with the Aldriches on the steam-yacht *Hermione*. She kept up her friendships, in person at South Berwick and in Boston, and by constant correspondence, and she kept on trying to write. Who knows whether, unimpaired, she might have surpassed the mark she set in *The Country of the Pointed Firs?* For one, I doubt it.

Twenty-five years after her death a poem, "Sarah Orne Jewett's Stories," by the late James Norman Hall, appeared in the *Atlantic Monthly*. From across the Pacific it celebrated "the folk Miss Jewett knew" and their houses:

> Just as they stood there many years ago
> A century from now it will be so!

To all this I make bold to add some lines of my own written more recently in California:

> Far, far away
> From Dunnet Landing, State of Maine,
> I held a book
> And breathed the pungent air of pointed firs
> Mixed with a salt sea breeze.
> Across a continent's expanse
> Could Dunnet Landing truly be so near?
>
> Yes, there it stands — small houses, weathered gray,
> Along a winding street,
> Lonely and weathered women and men,
> Fisher and farmer folk — a microcosm

WHO LIVED HERE?

Of all the larger ways of men writ small —
Beauty and bareness — scene and deed and word
All wrought together by the wand of art.

And she who held the wand,
That country doctor's daughter,
Learning her country in her father's chaise,
Learned also how to lead all minds and hearts
Through Down-East doorways into Down-East lives,
Till dwellers in great cities through the world
Dwelt thankfully in Dunnet Landing too.

Beauty and grace walked with her to the end,
Humor and kindness in her lovely face,
No more forgettable than the tales she told.

X

Longfellow and the Craigie House

WHEN LONGFELLOW had been living for ten years in Craigie House he wrote an unavailing petition to have the name of the street on which it stood changed from Brattle to Vassall. In the century before him it was called the King's Highway. The few houses on large pieces of land which lined it bore the name of Tory Row. Conspicuous among them was the house that became his own. It was built in 1759 by Henry Vassall of the family of opulent Jamaica planters, who quitted New England when the Revolution upset their order of things, but left notable traces behind them. One of these is an elaborate memorial in King's Chapel to two Vassalls who never lived here. A heraldic tombstone in the Christ Church graveyard in Cambridge is another. The oldest portion of the Adams Mansion in Quincy was built by a Vassall. This also was the maiden name of the wife of Thomas Oliver, who built Lowell's Elmwood. Longfellow's desire to revive the Vassall name, whatever might be said for that of Brattle, went well with the house in which he lived.

WHO LIVED HERE?

A greater name than Henry Vassall's came next in historic association with the house — the name of George Washington. For nearly a year from his taking command of the American army in Cambridge the Vassall house was his headquarters. The splendors of Tory days must have seemed to be returning when Mrs. Washington came from Virginia to join him, her coach drawn by four black horses, with postilions and servants in scarlet livery. Though Washington himself discouraged superfluous gaieties in the house, there was a Twelfth Night party during his occupancy. Longfellow, according to Howells, enjoyed telling a story of Washington in the Vassall house. One day, runs the tale, an aide-de-camp intruded upon him while he knelt in prayer. "He rebuked him," said Longfellow, "by throwing his scabbard at his head." It is of considerably greater moment that in this very house Washington directed the organization of his first army.

Between his quitting the Vassall house in 1776 and Longfellow's first entering it in 1837 more than sixty years intervened. In that period the house, with its surrounding hundred and fifty acres, became, after confiscation, the property in turn of Nathaniel Tracy of Newburyport, Thomas Russell of Boston, and, in 1791, of Andrew Craigie, whose activities as Apothecary-General of the Revolutionary Army and in various speculations had provided him with an ample fortune. He spent it lavishly both on the house itself and in the entertainment of guests. From the Philadelphia merchants Nalbro and John Frazer he enriched the place with all manner of beautiful furnishings, horses, wines, and cigars, and from that same center of good living imported even a cook. His hospitable bachelorhood ended with his marrying Elizabeth Nancy Shaw of Nantucket, left, through his later misfortunes, an impoverished and disillusioned turbaned widow, who maintained herself in what had come to be called Craigie House by renting rooms to Harvard students.

On an August day of 1837 Mrs. Craigie was visited by a most prepossessing and well-turned-out young man looking for lodgings. Though she had previously housed students who were to become Presidents of Harvard — Edward Everett and Jared Sparks — she was dubious about admitting another undergraduate, for such she took her applicant to be. It happened, however, that a copy of *Outre-Mer*, Longfellow's first book of general appeal, published only two years earlier, was lying on a table, near at hand, and when Mrs. Craigie learned that she was confronted by its author, the newly appointed Smith Professor of various languages, it was almost as if a T. S. Eliot blended with a Theodore Spencer had walked into a Cambridge dwelling house of recent years. Longfellow got the rooms he wanted, one of which had been occupied by Washington himself!

Who and what was this youthful-looking Smith Professor? If Longfellow had been called upon to account for himself to Mrs. Craigie, he might have told her that he was born at Portland, Maine, in 1807, graduated at Bowdoin College in 1825, and through the years since then had traveled and studied in Europe, taught at Bowdoin, and during his second sojourn abroad, for the further mastery of foreign languages before beginning to teach at Harvard, had suffered the loss of his youthful bride, Mary Storer Potter. The tale of what then befell him was to be told, for those who could read between the lines, in the first book he was to write in Craigie House — *Hyperion, a Romance.*

He had already published several textbooks on European languages, the translation of a Spanish poem, and *Outre-Mer,* a volume of sketches à la Washington Irving. *Hyperion,* written in what had been Washington's bedroom, appeared in 1839. In his recorded "Table-Talk" he is reported to have quoted a French proverb declaring it is not enough to be a great man — you must also come at the right time, and to this added, "This is particularly true of authors." It was certainly true of Longfellow, and the time at which he came, with *Hyperion* in special evidence of his coming, stands out the more clearly in retrospect through reading the romance in the two thinnish, austerely printed, plainly bound volumes of its first edition. The time is no less clearly suggested in the unblushing ro-

The Longfellow House — Cambridge, Massachusetts

The Poet's Study — Longfellow House

The West Parlor — Longfellow House

manticism of the book, only the more romantic for the frankly personal implications of the second volume.

Here a young bereaved traveler wandering about central Europe under the name of Paul Flemming encounters in Switzerland a beautiful, highly accomplished girl under the name of Mary Ashburton, with whom he falls desperately in love. They talk, discuss the drawings in her sketchbook, join in the translation of German poetry, but she will have none of him, and the tale ends in sadness. Longfellow of course knew that he was relating his own experiences with Miss Frances Appleton of Boston, traveling with her most prosperously placed family, and of course Miss Appleton, when she came to read the book, knew. The critics also seemed to know. One of the most responsible of them in Boston expressed his wonder that a man "could write a letter about his private life to a public on which he has as yet established no claim." The facts behind the avowed fiction might have been less obvious had not Longfellow himself pressed his suit so vigorously after his settlement in Cambridge. He resorted frequently to Boston for chance meetings with his "dark ladie" on the Common or, more deliberately, in the house of her father, Nathan Appleton, that faced it, and is now the upper half of the Boston Women's City Club. Nor was the suitor a figure at all likely to escape notice. His addiction to the smartest Paris and London clothes, his friendships with such livelier members of his own generation as

Felton — Dickens's "heartiest of Greek professors" — Charles Sumner, and Sam Ward in New York, added to his academic gown a clear color of town. To dispel the image of Fanny Appleton from his mind, he even tried to fall in love with one of the New York Sam Ward's sisters. Meanwhile his hopes in Boston were dashed again and again. Once in writing to a friend he alluded lightly to his late serious accident in Beacon Street. Again, after the lady passed him on a Cambridgeport street without recognition, he wrote in his journal, "It is ended." Yet it was not. At last Miss Appleton capitulated, and on July 13, 1843, seven years after their meeting in Switzerland, they were married. For a wedding gift she presented him with a charmingly bound copy of her European sketchbook, inscribed "Mary Ashburton to Paul Flemming." In more substantial recognition of the occasion Nathan Appleton presented the young couple with Craigie House and its surrounding land, which had shrunk from the many original Vassall acres to eight.

Longfellow's writing of *Hyperion* in Craigie House was only the beginning of its close identification with his wife. Before his marriage it was here he produced the poems, such as "A Psalm of Life," "The Wreck of the Hesperus," "The Village Blacksmith," "The Skeleton in Armor," and "Excelsior," which first evoked the general response that gave him his place among the most popular poets of his time wherever the English language was read or spoken. From his marriage in 1843 until his wife's tragic death eighteen years later in this very house, his domestic life, enriched by the birth of five children, made it the happiest of homes. Then, as Mrs. Longfellow in July of 1861 was sealing some boxes containing curls of their children's hair, a lighted match fell on her summer dress, which took fire, causing her death on the following morning. Longfellow himself was so burned in trying to save his wife that he could not attend her funeral at Mt. Auburn three days later, the anniversary of their wedding.

So much for Longfellow in his most intimate relationship with the house in which he lived. If it was a house of long-sustained romance, with joys offset by the deepest sorrows, it was also a house of many friendships and devoted labors of mind and spirit. Early in life Longfellow entered on the pursuits of a man of letters, and to those pursuits he remained constant to the end. When the routine of college teaching became irksome to him, he resigned his professorship — in 1854. As he had begun his writing career with translations, so in the years following the death of his wife he devoted himself to producing, in consultation with a congenial "Dante Club" of Cambridge neighbors, his English rendering of the *Divine Comedy*. Meanwhile in *Evangeline*, as early as 1846, in *The Song of Hiawatha* and *The Courtship of Miles Standish*, each in the decade of the fifties, and in a constant outpouring of other poetry, both narrative and lyrical, up to the very time of his death in 1881, he stood before his countrymen pre-eminently as their own beloved poet. The critics of his own time did not see so clearly as those of a later day that he was not to be counted among the great original thinkers of his time. It is no derogation to say that this would have been impossible for one whose work in largest measure was so derivative as his, so largely based upon reading, so little, in its major expressions, upon firsthand experience and observation. What it did possess, with exceptions above and below its average level, was the direct appeal of human sympathy, addressed in terms of metrical, amounting to musical, beauty, not to the sophisticated of the century beyond his own, but to readers of a hundred years ago who did not outgrow their simplicities of appreciation so early as their descendants, or the more vocal among them, have learned to do.

Longfellow the Poet is clearly to be read in his writings. Longfellow the Man is to be seen both in what he wrote and in his recorded relations with others. For witness to his outward appearance to them, many pictures of him may be studied. The schoolhouses of the land have familiarized successive generations of the young with the profuse white locks and beard framing the benevolent face in a picture which fixed in their minds for life the image of Poet. In earlier pictures he seems less a typical than an individual figure — of good looks and an air of personal distinction. In these he appears plainly as a person whose friendship would be sought and enjoyed, as indeed it was. Early and late the chosen spirits of Cambridge and Boston — his Bowdoin classmate Hawthorne, his accomplished, witty, brother-in-law "Tom" Appleton, Lowell, Norton, and in the younger generation Howells, to name but a few — were his intimates. The amenities of hospitality, dispensed and accepted, meant much to him. He dines with a small club at a friend's house, noting with satisfaction in his journal the "quails and canvas-back ducks," and adding, as early as 1848, "It seemed like the days gone by."

On a September day in 1877 he wrote in his journal, "Fourteen callers in the afternoon." From Dickens to Don Pedro he welcomed visitors from afar. For such an old friend as George W. Greene of Rhode Island Craigie House was a second home. It was to this friend he wrote in 1872, "I received the other day a valuable and curious present from England — namely Coleridge's inkstand; and only wish he had left some of his poems in it." Gifts and testimonials of many sorts flowed in from many sources — none more welcome, one may surely believe, than the armchair made from the "Village Blacksmith's" chestnut tree and presented to him on his seventy-second birthday by the schoolchildren of Cambridge.

It used to be told in Cambridge that one of Longfellow's grandchildren was taken to Rome as a little girl and after her first walk in the city exclaimed, mindful of a little street in her native town, "Why, there's an Appian Way in Rome, too!" If there is any basis of truth in this story it is only to be hoped that the exclamation was made while Longfellow could enjoy it. It was in Italy, and largely in Rome, that, at twenty-one, he set his face most resolutely toward such a lifetime as he passed, chiefly in the Cambridge of which he was so illustrious a citizen. To him perhaps more than to any other American of his period it was given especially to serve, through his writings in Craigie House, as a spiritual messenger between the Old World and the New.

XI

Lowell's Elmwood

WHEN JAMES RUSSELL LOWELL went to Europe in 1872 he left Thomas Bailey Aldrich in possession of his house at Cambridge, the "Elmwood" in which he was born and died. Writing to Aldrich from Paris in the spring of 1872 he said, "It is a pleasant old house, isn't it? Doesn't elbow one, as it were. It will make a frightful conservative of you before you know it. It was born a Tory and will die so. Don't get too used to it."

Born a Tory! The origin of the house gave abundant ground for this characterization. The builder and first occupant was a Tory of the first water, Thomas Oliver, of whom more in a moment. The house itself stood last in the procession known as Tory Row, on what was once called the King's Highway. Here were country houses of Boston merchants such as the Vassalls, with their substantial fortunes based on trade with the West Indies. There were two Vassall houses, one of which has now long been known as the Longfellow House. The Tory Row houses stood on large pieces of land, reaching, for those on the southerly side of the Highway, over gardens and fields, to the Charles River.

WHO LIVED HERE?

Thomas Oliver's wife was a Vassall, and he himself, born in Antigua, the island source of his family's wealth, had a family tie with Isaac Royall, whose mansion at Medford, with its slave quarters still standing, survives in witness to Tory grandeur in eighteenth-century New England. Oliver's house that came to be called Elmwood was built by him, it is said, in 1767. Even as late as 1875 Lowell could write from it, "I see the masts in the river and the spires in the town, and whatever noise of traffic comes to me now and then from the road but emphasizes the feeling of seclusion."

By that time the estate was greatly reduced from its original size of about a hundred acres. The seclusion found in it by Thomas Oliver, lieutenant governor of the Massachusetts Colony, was rudely broken as the Revolution approached. He was also president of the Massachusetts Council, by appointment usurped, as the colonists felt, by the King. His resignation of this post was demanded by an enraged multitude that thronged about his house on September 2, 1774. A committee presented a form of resignation for him to sign. The prospect of violence so distressed his family that he yielded, and wrote beneath the proffered form the following words with his signature: "My house at Cambridge being surrounded by four thousand people, in compliance with their commands I sign my name, Tho's Oliver."

So, after only seven years, the house born as Tory was

"Elmwood" — Cambridge, Massachusetts

The Upper Hallway — "Elmwood"

The Parlor — "Elmwood"

quitted by its first occupant, Tory both born and bred, who sought protection at once among the British forces in Boston. With them he sailed away to Halifax in March of 1776, and passed the rest of his life in England, except for visiting his properties in Antigua, where he took to himself a second wife. His Cambridge house, confiscated and used for a time as a camping-place for some of Benedict Arnold's men on their way to Ticonderoga, and as a hospital for wounded American soldiers, passed after a brief ownership by Andrew Cabot of Salem, to Elbridge Gerry, anything but a Tory. His name survives locally in "Gerry's Landing" on the Charles River, and more widely in the opprobrious "gerrymander," a word coined in 1812 when Gerry was Governor of Massachusetts and fathered the redistricting of a portion of Essex County for election purposes so that a map of the region could be drawn, perhaps by Gilbert Stuart, to resemble a salamander.

Before and during the Revolution Gerry, son of a prosperous Marblehead merchant, devoted his brains and his means to the American cause. He signed the Declaration of Independence, and became Vice-President of the United States under Madison. He had made himself exceedingly unpopular with the powerful class of Federalists in Massachusetts, and at one point so incurred the wrath of the people that his "Mansion House," as he called the subsequently named Elmwood, was again surrounded by a mob, which this time terrified his family by setting up a mock guillotine and showing the effigy of a headless man. When he died suddenly in Washington on his way to preside over the Senate as Vice-President, his fortune was so diminished that his family had to sell the Cambridge house with about ten surrounding acres. Its purchaser was the Reverend Charles Lowell, minister of the West Church in Boston, father of James Russell Lowell, who was born in the house February 22, 1819, only a year after his father acquired it.

The coincidence of Lowell's birthday with George Washington's was not a point to be missed by his celebrating friends. For his relation to Elmwood let us turn not so much to them as to words of his own, especially in his letters. Writing in 1844 to a friend who doubted the fitness of "Elmwood" as the name for the Lowell place, he boasted that he could show him "elms enough to vindicate the title we have given it" — the "we" establishing the name as a Lowell invention. Two years before his death he wrote from his study to another friend: "The two old English elms in front of the house haven't changed. The sturdy islanders! A little thicker in the waist, perhaps, as is the wont of prosperous elders, but looking just as I first saw them seventy years ago, and it is a balm to my eyes."

There is no trace of the elms in "Under the Willows," the poem that provided the title of a volume which his publishers wanted to call "Elmwood." But no, said Lowell: "It was throwing my sanctuary open and making a show-house of my hermitage."

Elms and willows were not the only trees at Elmwood. In a letter of July 4, 1876, Lowell recalled one of his very first remembrances of the place: "I remember how, fifty years ago to-day, I perched in a great oxheart cherry tree, long ago turned to mould, saw my father come home with the news of John Adams's death." Howells in his *Literary Friends and Acquaintances* has reported a remembrance of Lowell's, giving a year even before 1826: "He told me once of having been on a brief journey when he was six years old, with his father, and of driving up to the gate of Elmwood in the evening, and his father saying, 'Ah, this is a pleasant place! I wonder who lives here — what little boy?' "

He was still a boy when Thomas Wentworth Higginson, nearly four years younger, used to see him gallop on a white pony to the school, close to Elmwood, which they both attended. Nor was he much more than a boy, and presumably living at home, when shortly before his graduation at Harvard in 1838 he rose one day in the college chapel, bowing right and left in acknowledgment of the honor implied in his recent election as class poet, and giving such evidence of an injudicious celebration of this honor that he was rusticated to Concord till the Saturday before Commencement, and had to forego the reading of his own class poem. The feelings of his clerical father at this time are not recorded.

One suffering the father and son must have shared — the extreme cold of the Elmwood house in winter. In December of his senior year he wrote to a classmate, "You have not the most faint idea how cold it is up here at my parental mansion," and proceeded to particularize his "below zeroish sufferings." Many years later, in 1882, he inserted a parenthesis in a letter from London to his daughter: "(It will bring me home to you if I tell you that I have just been interrupted by a violent fit of sneezing and have shouted *Horatio!* half a dozen times just as your grandfather used, only without his prodigious force of lungs.)" It took Lowell's keen ear for dialect to render the sound of a sneeze as *Horatio*.

Lowell, as poet, essayist, scholar, and diplomatist has been so bewritten that in this place one cannot do better than stick close to his relations with Elmwood. There he lived on after quitting college, making his way especially as a writer for magazines. There he extended his range of writing, even, under the influence of his young wife, Maria White, to include the cause of antislavery, and to show himself less a conservative than he had been and was yet to become. When he was only twenty-nine, in 1848, he published his first series of *Biglow Papers*, his *Fable for Critics*, and two books of serious poetry. The old house teemed with production. Neither joys nor sorrows were lacking — in the births and deaths of children (only one of his four grew to maturity) and in the devastating loss of the wife of his youth. It would have been hard thereafter to untwine his heart from Elmwood.

He was still living there in 1857, when he became the first editor of the *Atlantic Monthly*, and made his second happy marriage, to Frances Dunlap. Already for two years he had held a professorship in Harvard College. The Elmwood setting was ideal for both editor and professor. There he could deal quietly with manuscripts, whether from other pens or his own, and there he could offer agreeable hospitalities to chosen contributors. Here is a story of his dealing with rejected manuscripts. One day as he crossed the Cambridge bridge, in walking to Boston, his hat blew into the Charles River. It was presumably a top hat, such as Barrett Wendell subsequently deplored Lowell's wearing at the same time with a short double-breasted jacket. It was stuffed with rejected manuscripts, which went to a watery grave, while a boatman rescued the hat. The *Atlantic* editorship had its humors, and when Lowell, after four years, half reluctantly gave it up, he wrote to his successor, James T. Fields, "I doubt if we see the finger of Providence so readily in the stoppage of a salary as in its beginning or increment." Yet he concluded gaily, "I have lost the *Atlantic*, but my cow has calved as if nothing had happened."

At Elmwood, whether as editor or as teacher, he appeared also as a pipe-smoker. Even out of doors, as he tells in *Under the Willows* of his encounter with a "dusty Tramp" —

> I bait him with my matches and my pouch,
>   Nor grudge the uncostly sympathy of smoke.

Indoors, Howells, whose friendship with Lowell began through *Atlantic* relationship, has told of their sitting before a wood fire after their weekly dinners together when "he smoked and talked. He smoked a pipe which was always needing tobacco, or going out, so that I have the figure of him before my eyes constantly getting up out of his deep chair to rekindle it from the fire with a paper lighter." Lowell's pipe figures also in the remembrance of Barrett Wendell, a Harvard undergraduate in the 1870's, repairing by night with fellow students to Elmwood for the reading and discussion of Dante under Lowell's guidance. In later years Wendell, in one place, wrote of him as the most inspiring teacher he had ever had; and in another as "the most human instructor ever vouchsafed Harvard youth — in '76." Henry Adams, an earlier pupil than Wendell, has told how he seized the chance to read with Lowell privately in his study, and has counted among the relatively few good points in his education the "good-natured encouragement" received from Lowell "to do what amused him." The Elmwood garden was no more a seedbed than its study.

LOWELL

Thoughts of the old place accompanied Lowell wherever he went. From Venice he wrote in 1873, "I long to go back to my reeking old den at Elmwood." When urged to live in Washington when his work as United States Minister in England came to an end, he wrote to a friend, "I have but one home in America, and that is the house where I was born and where, if it shall please God, I hope to die." His experience, rare in America, of birth, a long life, and death in the same house was shared with his lifelong friend, Charles Eliot Norton, first editor of his Letters, whose Shady Hill, at the opposite end of Cambridge from Elmwood, was comparable with it. Lowell had visited Europe more than once before his service as Minister, first to Spain, where his wife was desperately ill, and to England, where she died. Typical of the older order in America as Elmwood was, it was no more typical than Lowell himself, and his selection for the important diplomatic missions he held was recognized, both at home and abroad, as belonging to the very fitness of things.

It was no less fitting that his wish for his life to end where it began should be fulfilled. His final years were divided between the Englands, New and Old. Howells has reported a story of one of Lowell's latest returns to Elmwood, "sitting down in his old study, where he declared with tears that the place was full of ghosts." Let us not leave him thus, but in the mood of an earlier time when returning from a week's visit to Newport, he expressed his delight in finding "his own sponge hanging on its nail." Together with all the deeper meanings of Elmwood to him, this bit of domestic feeling should be remembered.

Nearly thirty years after Lowell's death in 1891, Arthur Kingsley Porter, a graduate of Yale, became Professor of Fine Arts at Harvard. Elmwood came not only into his possession but into its own again as a locus of the enduring influence of a stimulating teacher upon responsive pupils. Since Porter's death in 1933 the place has been occupied by his widow, whose researches in the early history of Elmwood have greatly enriched its accessible records. Elmwood will belong eventually to Harvard College.

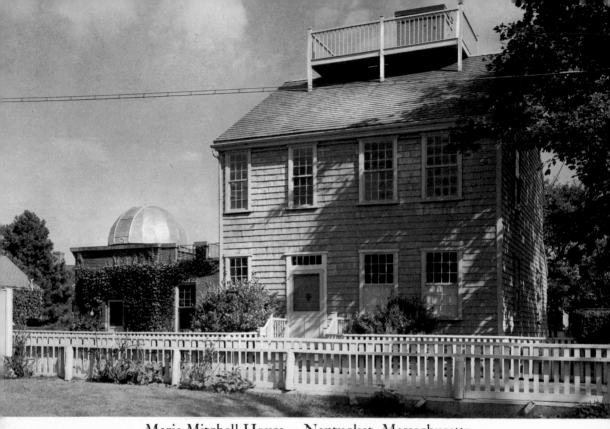

Maria Mitchell House — Nantucket, Massachusetts

West Façade — Maria Mitchell House

XII

Maria Mitchell: Sky-Sweeper

NOBODY can look far into the story of Nantucket Island without encountering the boy who wrote in a school composition, "Napoleon was a great man and a great soldier, but he was an off-islander." Now Maria Mitchell, until she reached the age of twenty-nine was very much an on-islander. Then she leaped suddenly into off-island, even international, fame by discovering a comet. A king of Denmark had offered a gold medal, to be valued at twenty ducats, to any first discoverer of a telescopic comet — that is, a comet not to be seen by the naked eye. To a successor on the Danish throne it was conclusively proved that the Nantucket discovery ante-dated, if only by two days, the same achievement by a noted astronomer in Rome, and to Maria Mitchell, hitherto not generally known even in America beyond the limits of her island, the medal was duly awarded. It seemed to have come out of a clear sky, but many portents had preceded it.

The ancestry and upbringing of Maria Mitchell conspired to produce something unusual, and apparently unique, since only one such woman emerged from conditions which she shared with many others. She was born August 1, 1818, in the small house on Vestal Street, now the Maria Mitchell Memorial, and here she lived for the first eighteen years of her life. She came of a line of Quakers, of whom the first settler on the Island, Thomas Macy, had sailed in 1659 with his family round Cape Cod in an open boat to escape the severities of Massachusetts toward members of his sect. The earliest Folger on the Island, from whom Benjamin Franklin was descended, was an ancestor also of Maria Mitchell. The surnames of both her parents are found in the following words in some old Nantucket rhymes about representative Island families: "The Mitchells good" and "A learned Coleman very rare." William Mitchell, her father, was notably good — and versatile. Before becoming cashier of the Pacific Bank in 1836, he followed a variety of callings, from farmer, cooper, soap-boiler, to schoolmaster and justice of the peace, all the while studying the heavens to such good purpose that he was appointed an astronomical observer for the Coast Survey.

William Mitchell's wife — Lydia Coleman before her marriage — was a more austere adherent to the Quaker faith. "She could not have lied," said her husband, "to save the life of a child." It was the father, not the mother, of the eleven Mitchell children, of whom Maria was the third, who upheld his lively daughters in bringing a piano — a demoralizing instrument in Quaker eyes — into the little house on Vestal Street. The simple basis of his own religious faith is suggested by his saying that "an undevout astronomer is mad."

Maria Mitchell herself was of too independent a spirit to accept meekly the Quaker discipline. Indeed while still a girl she informed the authorities of her Meeting that "her mind was not settled on religious subjects," and she was accordingly disowned as a Friend. Retaining the "plain language" for family use, she satisfied herself with Unitarian affiliations, though refraining from church membership. In later life, when obliged at Vassar and elsewhere to listen to many sermons with which she could not at all agree, she was credited with remarking, "It is strange that people who go to church are no worse than they are." Formalities meant so little to her that when she visited Rome in Holy Week of 1858 she wrote, "I stayed [at St. Peter's] five hours to-day to see the Pope wash feet, which was very silly, for I saw mother wash them much more effectively twenty years ago."

Nantucket, through the far-ranging interests of its whaling captains and lesser seamen, was a place of wide horizons. Youngsters who would have learned the catechism elsewhere were here taught to box the compass. So pervasive, however, were the ways of Quakerism that the name of Robinson Crusoe could be coupled with that of "his good man, Sixth Day." The extensive and the intensive were joined in a special local atmosphere.

In the course of Maria Mitchell's schooling, beginning in dame schools and including instruction from the Reverend Cyrus Peirce, yet to become head of the first normal school in America, she attended the school of her own father, who justified his title of "William the Teacher" by such injunctions to his pupils as this: "Thee must wonder; thee must watch closely, then thee will see and know for thyself." That was precisely what he was teaching his daughter Maria at home. While she was still hardly more than a child she began helping him with his astronomical studies, pursued with simple instruments — telescope, sextant, chronometer — on the "whale-walk" above the Vestal Street house. Beneath William Mitchell's record of hours, minutes, and seconds in an eclipse in February ("2 mo.") 1831, the following note, obviously written in later years, is found: "This time was noted by me; I was 12½ years old. M. M."

It could not have been far from this time that she gave another juvenile demonstration of her capacities. The Nantucket sea-captains, before setting forth on long voyages, used to bring their chronometers to William Mitchell to be "rated" — that is, to have their variation from true time accurately ascertained. One day when the trusted "rater" was away from home a captain, on the point of sailing, brought his chronometer to the Vestal Street house, and was about to depart disappointed by Mrs. Mitchell's report of her husband's absence, when little Maria broke in, "I can do it, Mother, I'm sure I can, if thee'll only let me try. Thee knows I have often watched Father." Mother and sea captain yielded to her plea, and with the coming of night she proved her competence for the undertaking.

After one year in "Father Peirce's" school as a pupil and another year as his assistant, Maria Mitchell, in 1835, opened a school of her own for girls at the modest cost of $3.00 a quarter per pupil. Her own education took what was perhaps its longest forward step when, in 1837, she became librarian of the Nantucket Athenæum, a post which she held for seventeen years. The library was open only on weekday afternoons and Saturday evenings. For its patrons she took pains to acquire books rather above than below their common level of intelligence, and over some of these she exercised a censorship which withheld them from general circulation yet kept them available for the inspection of large-minded trustees. For the development of her own powers the Athenæum, in the many hours of every day through which the library was not open to the public, presented extraordinary advantages. Its shelves were well stocked with the works of higher mathematics indispensable to that mastery of astronomy of which the navigators of Nantucket stood in special need. To these books Maria Mitchell applied herself with all the vigor of her strong intellect.

In the year before her librarianship began her father

became cashier of the Pacific Bank, and the Mitchell family moved from the little house on Vestal Street to live in the spacious upper rooms of the bank building, which holds an association with her quite as important as that of her birthplace and early home.

It was on the roof of the Pacific Bank that she made the discovery mentioned in the first of the preceding paragraphs, and woke up, like Byron, to find herself famous. On the night of October 1, 1847, she was at her customary "sweeping" when a strange phenomenon in the skies struck her vision. Her father was entertaining guests downstairs. To him, her preceptor and colleague — for was not she too an astronomical observer for the Coast Survey? — she hurried and begged him to come "up scuttle," as they had said in Vestal Street, to confirm or refute her observation. He found it so valid that he reported it at once to the Harvard Observatory, where the astronomers William C. and George P. Bond, father and son, were the Mitchells' good friends. "If you are going to find any more comets," George Bond soon wrote to "Dear Maria," "can you not wait until they are announced by the proper authorities? At least don't kidnap such another as this last one."

To qualify, on the grounds of priority, for the royal Danish medal, Maria Mitchell became the subject of a considerable correspondence, both European and transatlantic, in which Edward Everett, then President of

Harvard, took an important part. "It would be pleasant," he wrote, while the award was still under consideration, to George Bancroft, his successor as American Minister to Great Britain, "to have the Nantucket girl carry off the prize from all the greybeards and observatories in Europe." In due time her claim was officially recognized, and the medal came to her at Nantucket.

Nearer home she received another recognition — election, in 1848, to the American Academy of Arts and Sciences. She was the first woman chosen to this learned body, and after more than a hundred years it can be said that she was the first of only twelve out of the multitude of Fellows elected to the Academy since its beginning in 1780. The word "Fellow," as applied to Maria Mitchell, was too much for the secretary of the Academy at the time of her election, the eminent Harvard botanist, Asa Gray; and he is said to have registered his personal protest by substituting "Honorary Member" for "Fellow" in the Academy's definition of her status.

In the very nature of this little book, designed to associate names and persons with local habitations, Maria Mitchell is not to be followed at all closely from her Nantucket planting and flowering into the fruition of her later years. Neither before nor since 1850 could it be said that any other Nantucket Islander has become in the largest sense so much an off-Islander. In her case this came about through widely extended personal relationships, especially with the learned, and through travel in both America and Europe. These experiences are amply described in the too scrupulously screened letters edited by her sister, and in the recent biography, *Sweeper in the Sky,* by Helen Wright, to which this brief sketch is much beholden.

Let it suffice to say in this place that from the first blazing of her own star into public notice she remained at Nantucket, deeply devoted to her invalided mother until her death, after which she moved, in 1859, with her father to Lynn, Massachusetts, where a married sister was living. There the astronomical Mitchells set up a little observatory in the yard beside their house, and occupied themselves happily with the stars. This was not to last long. For several years before Vassar College opened its doors in 1865 Maria Mitchell was under pressure to become one of its original small faculty as Professor of Astronomy. At last she yielded, and held the post till Christmas of 1888, only six months before her death.

"Strong-minded" is a term less commonly applied to women today than it was before their objects of higher education and political equality were so largely attained. The term must have been used freely in relation to a woman astronomer who was also a formidable figure in the movement for Women's Rights. Yet there is abundant evidence that in her love of children, flowers, and poetry, in her humor, and in the influence of her character as well as her intellect upon her pupils at Vassar, there

The Front Parlor with Maria Mitchell's Telescope

The Old Kitchen — Maria Mitchell House

were qualities to which the word "formidable" would not in the least apply.

Her portrait as a ringleted old lady explains the conclusion of a railroad newsboy who thought she might be Harriet Beecher Stowe or Elizabeth Cady Stanton and on learning that she was Maria Mitchell exclaimed, "I knowed you be somebody!" Another portrait, painted at her telescope, in her early thirties, shows a mid-Victorian young woman of considerable personal charm. The ample printed records of her life give no indication of her exercising this charm in any masculine direction, or of any romantic interest in her on the part of a man. If any such interest existed on either side, the reticence of her period might fully account for any failure to mention it. But why seek to find in Maria Mitchell anything beyond a high examplar of devotion to womanhood and to science? "Born a woman — " she wrote, as she approached sixty — "born with the average brain of humanity — born with more than the average heart — if you are mortal, what higher destiny could you have?"

XIII

The Lifetime Ride of
Paul Revere

THERE cannot be many New Englanders painted by Copley in early life and by Stuart in old age. A portrait by either one of these artists is counted a patent of high respectability where patents of nobility do not exist. There are two such portraits of Paul Revere. They would serve well as illustrations of the first and last chapters of an American Success Story.

The Copley portrait shows its subject at about the age of thirty, in his shirt sleeves, gripping with a vigorous left hand a round, sturdy teapot of the sort he was then making. The graver's tools appear on the table supporting the right elbow. The firm right hand holds the firm chin of a square, determined face — that of an artisan, rather than one of the more favored class usually pictured by Copley. For *artisan*, as suggesting another class, let us, in this instance, say rather *artificer*, for the portrait may well have been painted in payment for small objects, such as silver frames for miniatures, made for Copley by Revere.

The Stuart portrait was painted in 1813, when Revere was seventy-eight years old. His second wife, Rachel

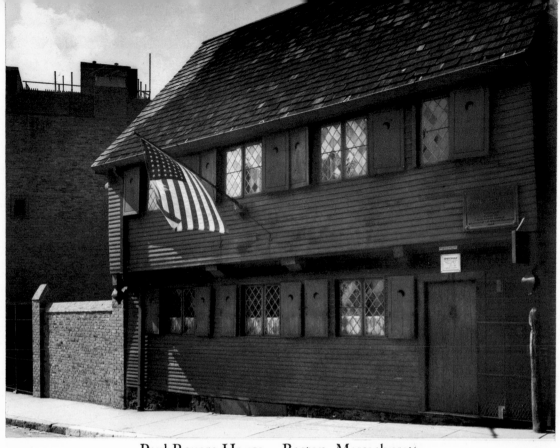

Paul Revere House — Boston, Massachusetts

The Rear Wing — Paul Revere House

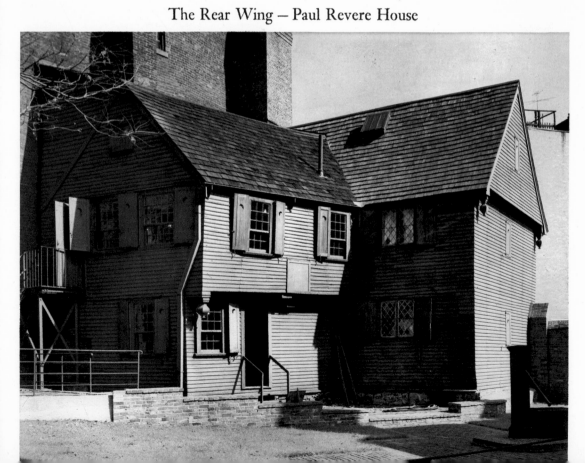

PAUL REVERE

Walker Revere, was painted by Stuart at the same time, on order of their eldest son, Joseph Warren Revere, his father's business partner in the prosperous manufacture of copper. Here the young artificer has grown, with a shrewd and kindly look, into one of those distinguished old Boston magnates who sat for Stuart — and Mrs. Revere, with only two weeks more to live, appears his proper matronly consort.

Over against these two Paul Reveres in portraiture, there are two others, one in song, one in story — the abbreviated word for history. The Paul Revere of song has the advantage, at least in that fame which in broad rumor lies. Longfellow's "Midnight Ride" made him a great legendary figure. He took for the theme of his poem one of the most picturesque incidents in the whole of the Revolutionary War, and if he could have had the benefit of reading *Paul Revere and the World He Lived In*, by Esther Forbes (1942) — now an indispensable, and enjoyable, book for every student of its subject — he would not have placed Revere on "the opposite shore," but in Boston, when the two lanterns were hung in the Christ Church tower, and he would not have carried his rider all the way to Concord, but only to Lexington, where the British stopped him. It matters not that he missed these and some lesser points of interesting detail. He told the essential story, and fixed the fame of his hero. This was not accomplished by an earlier bard, the Reverend John

Pierpont, whose fame in poetry is now eclipsed by his grandson's in finance. Longfellow, whatever his omissions, was guiltless of any two such lines as these of Pierpont's:

> While midnight wraps him in her mantle dark,
> Halts at the house of Reverend Mr. Clark.

The story needs no retelling here. Let us see rather what preceded and followed it in the longer ride of Paul Revere through life.

His father, Apollos Rivoire, a French Huguenot silversmith, came to Boston in the winter of 1715–1716, and in 1729 married Deborah Hitchbourn, of vigorous New England stock. To fit his name to his new surroundings he changed it to Paul Revere. Paul and Apollos were closely enough conjoined in Scripture to warrant this transition. The change from Rivoire to Revere, he said, was merely "on account that the Bumpkins pronounce it easier." Such was the Boston way with Huguenot names — Baudouin into Bowdoin, Faneuil, in common parlance if not in spelling, into Funnel. Could New England have done better than the South with Huger?

Paul Revere, the second of his parents' nine children, was born in December of 1735. From a house on his grandfather Hitchbourn's Wharf his parents moved, when he was only eight, to another at the head of the nearby Clark's Wharf, where his father practiced his trade of silversmith and the younger Paul continued it until, in 1770, he acquired the house in North Square which now stands as his memorial.

This house, occupied for most of the years between 1770 and 1800 by Paul Revere and his considerable family, is said to be the only standing example of a seventeenth-century dwelling in a large American city. Between its building, about 1680, and its restoration in 1908 it underwent many changes, including the addition of a third story. Its present form is believed to be that in which the Reveres occupied it. In 1800 they were established in a larger house on Charter Street, at the corner of the present Hanover Street.

To return to Paul Revere's beginnings, for a few years the water-front boy attended the North Writing School. The more advanced Latin School teaching was not for an artisan's boy soon to be apprenticed to his father's trade. He learned better how to figure and write than to spell. As a boy of his neighborhood he joined with thrifty mates in a youthful Society of Bell-Ringers, paid to ring and care for the peal of bells in the spire of the very Christ Church in which lanterns were yet to be hung for him.

Before coming of age Paul Revere had gone far in developing his skill and taste as a silversmith. Nor was this all. He began copper-plate engraving, from designs of others, and for a few years practiced dentistry, as the skill was then pursued. This was chiefly in replacing lost teeth with substitutes carved from ivory or adapted from the teeth of animals, and fastened with gold or silver wires, or with silk. When the body of General Joseph Warren, hastily buried after his death at Bunker Hill, was exhumed, Paul Revere could identify it by two teeth he had himself wired. Both as engraver and as dentist Paul Revere was more artificer than artisan. In reference to his beautiful creations in silver, each of these words may be transmuted to *artist*.

His versatility was by no means confined to the handicrafts he practiced. At one point, in 1783, he broke new ground, for him, by opening a general store, offering to the public all manner of miscellaneous objects, from fish lines and playing cards to spectacles and plated silver. To follow him in any detail through the years immediately before and after the outbreak of war with Britain would relate him to the whole spirit of revolt in Boston. In his quiet, competent way, he associated himself with all objectors to the English rule. Thus he entered into close relations with Joseph Warren, Sam Adams, and other leaders, and he led in the "organized mobs" of the time and place. As a Mason, a member of clubs and caucuses, a Son of Liberty, and a witness of the "Massacre," a participant in the "Boston Tea Party," he prepared himself for any service he could render to the American cause. One line of the "Rallying Song of the Tea-Party" that was promptly produced, "Our Warrens three and bold Revere," gave him the adhesive name of "Bold Revere" — a designation he might already have won through a street fist-fight, incurring a court fine, with a cousin by marriage. It was immediately after the "Party" that Revere made his first recorded ride of importance — to carry to the Committee of Correspondence in Philadelphia the news of that momentous event. There were several later such exploits in the saddle, besides the one celebrated by Longfellow.

The Midnight Ride stands at the apex of Paul Revere's common fame. Before it occurred he had married twice, first Sara Orne, by whom he had eight children, and then Rachel Walker, who bore him eight more. Of all the sixteen only one of the first marriage and four of the second survived him. In the year before his first marriage, in 1757, he had a brief military experience as second lieutenant in a colonial British regiment in the expedition against the French at Crown Point and Ticonderoga. In the Revolution he had Massachusetts commissions as both major and lieutenant-colonel, and in the second capacity had command of Castle Island. He saw some service also with the army in Rhode Island and Maine, but the by-products of war were more to his mind than war itself. The planning of a powder mill and the casting of cannon were his natural contributions to the cause of the new country. When the British man-of-war *Somerset* was wrecked on a Cape Cod shore, there was a poetic justice in the appointment of Paul Revere, who had skirted her "huge black bulk" as he was rowed from Boston to Charlestown on the famous April night, to salvage her big guns for American use. This he did, to the number of twenty-one brass cannon. Here was but one instance of his all-round American know-how.

From the casting of cannon during the war to the casting of bells after it was another natural transition of interest and achievement. Before his time the art of bell-making was little known and practiced in America. Revere was not an actual pioneer in the field, but when the Second Church, combining the Old North and the Cockerel, needed to replace the cracked bell of the Old North, Paul Revere, skilled in the making of small and large objects in metal, was commissioned to undertake the work, and produced a bell bearing its own description, "The first bell cast in Boston 1792. P. Revere." His son, Joseph Warren Revere, a boy of fifteen at this time, was early associated with his father in the making of bells and kept it up after Paul Revere's death — with the result of producing in all about four hundred bells, hung not only in New England but even so far afield as in Canada and Cuba.

With the uses of another metal for purposes both of peace and of war, Revere began to busy himself before the century to which he belonged, the eighteenth, was over. This metal was copper, serviceable in various ways in the

The Old Kitchen — Paul Revere House

Fireplace in the Front Room — Paul Revere House

Upstairs Bedroom – Paul Revere House

building and outfitting of the many vessels turned out by the Boston shipyards. When the infant navy of the United States began to build such ships as the *Constitution* and *Essex* in Boston, Paul Revere was on hand with offers — accepted — to provide their copper-work from his own newly constructed mill at Canton. At first he was not ready to sheathe these vessels, but by 1803, when the *Constitution* was reconditioned, Revere could provide the copper sheathing for her hull. Had he not already supplied the sheathing for the dome of the new State House, not to be gilded until Revere had been long in his grave?

In the development of this copper business his son, Joseph Warren Revere, became his partner, his mainstay, and successor. He lived on until 1868, by which time Revere Copper had taken an important place in American industry — a place secured and enlarged through the merging, under later Reveres, with other copper-manu-facturing interests throughout the country.

On the same land in Canton with the copper mill stood a dwelling house which Revere called Canton Dale, and occupied except for the winter months spent at the Charter Street house in Boston. He celebrated this country residence in a long piece of homely verse, suggesting that he could entertain the harmless day as comfortingly to himself as a seventeenth-century poet, or that more recent occupant of the home where never is heard a discouraging word — verses glowing with the same domestic satisfaction and general content with things as they had come to be. If he could sit for Stuart while the War of 1812 was still in progress, he could also join, in his eightieth year, with "Mechanics of the Town of Boston" in erecting earthworks, each with his own shovel, against the day of an expected British attack by sea.

His final circumstances and surroundings were such as the most industrious apprentice of the 1740's could hardly have imagined. As he looked back from Canton Dale over his long, eventful span of years, he could not have reproached himself with any lack of energy, any failure to make the most of opportunities, fortuitous or planned. His career may be called, with no silly flapping of eagles' wings, typically American. On May 10, 1818, his ride through the years came to its end.

Old Occupants

A Postscript

Come summer, let the sunshine pour
Through windows up and wide-flung door!
Come winter, turn the precincts bright
With logs aflame and candlelight!
In every season, come what may,
Give heed to what the echoes say,
Listen for footsteps from the past,
Note curiously the shadows cast
By presences that once were here
And now all dimly reappear!
These may have read on life's long page
The secrets of our heritage,
And in their whispers might be heard
Some waited, all-explaining word.
From mystic spaces where they roam
Greet them as wanderers come home!
Give place to all such visitants —
Perhaps immortal occupants!